Blue Ribbon Sampler

by Olwyn Horwood

GPL GEORGESON PUBLISHING LIMITED

Publisher's Note

The designs in this book were made using fabric and threads available in retail shops in New Zealand. As publisher, we are aware that some of these items may not be found in your local shops, so every effort has been made to include and suggest alternative materials that can be found in your country. We believe and know that the alternatives suggested will give very satisfactory results, and most importantly in the end, your own masterpiece to enjoy! As always we welcome your letters, email messages and telephone calls. The messages we receive from everywhere needlework is enjoyed brighten our day! Please let us know your progress with this Sampler.

Prue Georgeson

Published by Georgeson Publishing Limited

P.O. Box 100-667, North Shore Mail Centre, New Zealand 1330.
Ph: 649 410 2079 Fax: 649 410 2069
Email: gpl@georgeson.co.nz Web site: www.georgeson.co.nz

ISBN 0-9582105-3-5

© (2000) Georgeson Publishing Limited

Editor:	Prue Georgeson
Photography:	Maria Sainsbury
Illustrations and Layout:	Thinking Caps Visual Communications and Andreena Buckton of Noodle Design Corp
Printed:	Hong Kong

Acknowledgements

I would like to pay a special tribute to my husband Len who encouraged and supported me every step of the way as I was working on this book and my first book *From My Hands*. I will miss his support greatly.

Olwyn Horwood

Contents

Introduction

Once Upon A Band
Nine Samplers in One or One Sampler with Nine Parts!

Once Upon a Band was stitched to give me the opportunity to use some of the many border patterns I have collected over the years. I have stitched numerous Samplers of varying styles but these have still not given me the opportunity to use all of the patterns that I have admired. Samplers are a needlework tradition from across Europe as well as England and in admiring a Spanish Sampler worked in 1756 by Dona Isabel Eulogia de la Espade I had the inspiration for this Sampler.

Once Upon a Band is a happy combination of a layout inspired by Dona Isabel's Spanish Sampler combined with bands from the English embroidery tradition. Each of the nine sections could be a sampler in itself, please refer to page 40 for more information on this.

Traditionally the border patterns used in Samplers were not stitched from patterns nor were they centred, rather the needle woman would see a design and copy it, starting it at one edge and finishing it when she ran out of material! This gives a charming and less formal appearance to the Sampler and you will see this is how I have stitched my patterns.

I designed this Sampler to be attractive from every angle. The centre features two verses one to be read from the top and one to be read from the bottom. The motifs in the centre are stitched half facing up and the other half facing down. The band patterns can happily be viewed from any angle.

The two verses I used are shown on the appropriate chart. As well I give an upper and lower case alphabet so that you can use alternative verses if you prefer.

My friends know that I have a deep love of Samplers and I felt I wanted to include some of the historical features of earlier Samplers which have charmed and delighted me and have made Samplers a much loved form of needlework. One feature is the narrow repeating border right round the outside of this Sampler. Inside this border each of the four sides has a different floral design. They are all of a similar width but give the Sampler a less structured appearance.

Each section across the top and bottom of the sampler features a range of band patterns that I chose from my personal collection to compliment each other. They come from many different sources. I have worked with a reasonably limited colour palette to ensure the different bands blended into a harmonious whole. They are all designs that have been used in earlier embroideries. There are a number of different carnation borders - carnations have featured in Samplers since the seventeenth century. Strawberries are also popular as are pomegranates, chrysanthemums, acorn oak and leaf, tulips, grapes, rose, pansies fig, pineapples plus many more. Exotic and familiar flora to the needleworker of the seventeenth century.

The author stitching in her lounge.

The two side middle panels were inspired by the white work panels usually found in seventeenth century band samplers. There are six different border patterns with the bottom area featuring filet embroidery. Full instructions are given for this. Alternative satin stitch designs, which could be used in the area featuring filet embroidery, are also given.

The sampler is finished with a narrow hem worked in antique hem stitch and mitred corners.

I loved stitching this sampler and hope you feel the same pride and pleasure with your finished Sampler as I do with mine.

Happy stitching!

History of Samplers

An Introduction

21 x 90cm
Whitework Sampler
stitched by author.
Similar in style to those
worked in England in
the 17th and 18th
Century.

Samplers.

These small pieces of cloth, embroidered with a variety of designs, have survived centuries and still inspire, interest and enthuse the modern embroiderer. Samplers have been around not just for hundreds of years but thousands. The earliest surviving example of what is thought to be a Sampler is a Peruvian Sampler which has been approximately dated between AD200 and 500. Fragments of decorated material have also been found in the tombs of ancient Egyptians and dated around AD400-500.[1]

The word Sampler is derived from the Latin word 'exemplum' meaning 'something chosen from a number of things, a sample ... an example to be followed, a model'[2].

The Sampler is one of the most important types of textile work because it shows exactly how the different kinds of stitch patterns were worked. Samplers were made and kept as a record of particular patterns just as we use books today. The material was hand spun from flax then woven into narrow bands, the size of the loom determining the width of the linen. They varied in width from 15 - 40 cms (6 - 16 in) and this was wide enough to work one big pattern, or repeats of a smaller pattern.

Material was very precious and therefore every inch was used. This meant that little thought was given to the placement of patterns and they were stitched where they would fit. The selvages were used as edging with a narrow hem at the top and bottom. Some samplers had the edges bound with ribbon as a sort of bias binding, with bows decorating the corners. Either way early needleworkers were very economical in their use of material. When not in use they were rolled up for safe keeping. This record was preserved for future reference for the original stitcher and also for future generations. They are mentioned in housekeeping records, inventories and wills. Later when their intrinsic value was recognised they were framed to preserve and display as valued family artifacts.

The stitching on the Samplers was worked with silk threads in many colours. Sometimes up to twenty different colours were used on one piece of embroidery. The range of shades available was increased by twisting together strands of two different colours. Some Samplers stitched used silver and gold threads as well as pearls.

We do not have Samplers from the early years of the reign of Elizabeth I or before, yet the work from the later part of her reign is confident and colourful, full of vitality and impressive technical competence. The Renaissance movement of the late fifteenth and early sixteenth centuries brought a strong revival in all forms of the decorative arts but without printed patterns available the best method for recording patterns for future use was in the creation of samplers.

Dressmaking and needlearts were the concern of all girls and women other than the poorest members of the population. It was particularly the concern of high-ranking ladies who were very well educated in Latin and Greek, modern languages as well as proficiency in spinning, needlework and music.[3] The stitch repertoire of the Elizabethan embroiderer was formidable, the level of technical expertise of these early Samplers excites our respect and admiration.

Traditionally Samplers were stitched as a record of patterns. Even with the arrival of pattern books, which were a great inspiration for the needleworker, many needleworkers did not have access to these.

The earliest known dated and signed Sampler is the now well known sampler stitch by Jane Bostocke for Alice Lee dated 1596. Worked as a pattern record with spot motifs placed haphazardly this was the style of Sampler worked at the beginning of the seventeenth century.

As the century developed the samplers more commonly featured several rows of border patterns and alphabets worked in coloured silks and using a large number of different stitches, referred to now as a Band Sampler. Sometimes a verse was interspersed with the different bands. From the 1650's more samplers included a religious or moral verse and it is considered that this may point to the lessening importance of the Sampler as a record of patterns and to its increasing importance as a learning exercise.

24 x 66cm
Band Sampler stitched by author in the style of 17th century English Band Samplers. The two figures at the base of the sampler appear in many samplers stitched in coloured silks and also in cutwork techniques throughout the 17th and 18th centuries. The design was first published in Baroque Charted Designs for Needlework 1604.

42 x 45cm
Sampler worked by the author in the style of Spanish Samplers of the 18th Century. It is colourful and covered with densely worked patterns.

Many featured cut, drawn and lace work patterns across the lower portions of the Band Sampler. Others feature only cut and drawn white work. Portraits of the period frequently show amazing and very deep ruffs with finely worked lace edgings - these were probably the work of professional embroiderers. The lace patterns which feature in the band samplers were probably used on smaller items of clothing such as baby caps and night caps and as edgings on handkerchiefs and cuffs.

Samplers were important in other parts of Europe at this time also and each country developed a style of its own. In Germany they were a similar shape to the English but tended to be worked in two styles; either they had a simple floral border surrounding a number of small geometric motifs placed at random or they included alphabets and border patterns plus randomly placed motifs. Belgian Samplers were similar to the German style but a greater variety of stitches was used. Dutch Samplers had a similar subject matter but were square or wider than they were long. The French and Italian Samplers of the period tended to be square and whereas the French Sampler was worked almost entirely in cross stitch, the Italian Sampler included other stitches plus cut and drawn work - more similar to the English. Scandanavian Samplers tended to have extensive drawn thread work.

Samplers were also being made in Mexico and Spain, and these were usually on a larger scale and worked with very brightly coloured silks.

The appearance of the eighteenth century English Sampler is quite different. It became a 'picture' with a purpose! The shape changed from the long narrow band sampler to a squarer shape - more suitable for framing. Borders appeared at first on only two sides but gradually this spread to three and then all four sides. There were more open spaces between the embroidered flowers and animals and the inclusion of a verse was almost universal. Most Samplers were now made in schools so alphabets and numerals were included rather than the latest and newest stitch techniques.

Samplers had been worked on linen but in the eighteenth century this changed, and some were worked on a fine woolen cloth until it was realised just how susceptible this was to moths. By the end of the century most Samplers were again worked on linen.

With the development of the pictorial Sampler came the inclusion of houses, and landscape scenes along with families. These were generally shown on the lower half of the sampler. Some particularly attractive American Samplers from this time featured local buildings of note surrounded by an attractive floral border and are a delight to view. The verses that featured in these Samples were frequently dedicated to the parents of the stitcher thanking them for their care. Many verses were religious in content.

Near the end of the eighteenth century some rather different Samplers appeared. Map Samplers were popular and are now a most interesting source of study. The map could cover a very small area or district or conversely it could include the two hemispheres albeit most inaccurately. Darning samplers also became more fashionable, possibly in response to the need to repair the damask tableclothes now available. Whilst these were extremely practical they could also be most decorative. There were samplers featuring hollie point which showed a high level of technical skill not so evident in the other samplers of this period. Other 'novelty' Samplers also became popular in this period including, Almanacs, rebus and acrostic samplers.

By the end of the eighteenth century the technical expertise so evident in the Samplers of the seventeenth century was no longer obvious. The shape and purpose of the Sampler had also changed.

The Sampler of the nineteenth century was different again. It was a functional piece of embroidery on which to learn techniques. There were a small number of pattern books intended for children and especially printed for the purpose. They were made almost entirely of cross stitch, often in wool rather than silk though they did feature some of the plants motifs and borders loved by earlier embroiderers these Samplers were not the vibrant visual delight of the earlier Samplers.

The twentieth century was a period of huge change. Major global conflicts and the development of industry and different working conditions in the Western world mean that needlework was no longer a necessity. Machines and mass production have removed the need for time consuming and often tedious sewing of clothing and underwear leaving the modern embroiderer the luxury of choosing to stitch yet despite all these changes Samplers still hold a place dear in our hearts!

18 x 21cm
Sampler supplied by author featuring Adam & Eve with the serpent, a motif that appeared on Samplers in England & Europe from the 17th-19th centuries.

1   Synge L. Editor, *The Royal School of Needlework Book of Needlework and Embroidery*, Wm Collins Sons & Co Ltd, London, 1986.

2   Sebba A, *Samplers: Five Centuries of a Gentle Craft*, Weidenfeld and Nicholson, London, 1979.

3   Digby G W, *Elizabethan Embroidery*, Faber and Faber, London, 1963.

Requirements

21 x 30cm
This band sampler features different pomegranate designs popular in Samplers from the 17th-19th centuries.

Fabric - Linen

The best fabric for cross stitch and Samplers was, and still is, linen. It is a fabric that has been used to make Samplers for hundreds of years. It is long lasting and is not attractive to moths and similar thread eating insects. It has stood the test of time and when stitching a design that is going to take many hours to create it is important to buy materials worthy of your time and effort in creating, what will be, a masterpiece and heirloom for your home.

When you buy the linen for this Sampler check that it is woven in such a way that there is a gap between each thread. This will make your counting so much easier. Two linens can have the same thread count but be woven quite differently giving one a dense appearance and the other with threads that can be individually counted quite easily. The latter linen is the one to choose for working a Sampler of this kind. (I used Charles Craft 35 count unbleached linen.) There are many suitable linens available. Check the fabrics available at your favourite needlework store and choose a linen that you personally find easy to count and with a thread count you enjoy working with. We give the quantity of fabric to buy for linen with a thread count from 28 - 35 threads per inch and all will create a Sampler that will give you lasting satisfaction and pride.

Linen

Threads per inch	Finished Size	Linen
35	61 x 69 cm 24 x 27 in	81 x 89 cm 32 x 35 in
32	66 x 74 cm 26 x 29 in	86 x 94 cm 34 x 37 in
31	69 x 77 cm 27 x 30 in	89 x 97 cm 35 x 38 in
30	71 x 79 cm 28 x 31 in	91 x 99 cm 36 x 39 in
28	77 x 84 cm 30 x 33 in	97 x 104 cm 38 x 41 in

A range of 19th century needlework tools.

You may prefer to select one or two sections of Once Upon a Band and stitch a smaller sampler. To do this refer to **How to Stitch Once Upon a Band as a Smaller Sampler** page 40.

Threads

To create this Sampler I selected a palette of approximately 30 different colours. This gives a good range and working in a chosen palette means that all the different pattern bands blend together well.

I personally like to choose a colour range of medium strength colours and then include darker and lighter highlights. It is easier to work successfully in the middle range of colours than it is with all dark or all light tones. I stitched this Sampler using DMC stranded cottons. The numbers for these threads plus Anchor and Madeira threads are given. Only one thread of stranded cotton is used for all cross stitch.

Threads used in this Sampler

- *Thread for self coloured borders*
  Coton a broder 16 and 25 medium mole 642, plus stranded cottons listed below

- *Thread for Hem stitch*
  The hemstitch was worked using matching DMC natural cotton (40) 642. There are a wide range of alternative threads that could be used including Madeira Cotona (50) Au Ver a Soie 1003, Zwicky 100 % cotton or silk, Gutermann 100% cotton or silk and Dewhurst Sylko.

Modern needlework accessories.

• *Threads for cross stitch and satin stitch*

Colours to buy	DMC	Anchor	Madeira	No. of Skeins
medium Paris pink	223	895	0812	1
medium plum pink	316	1017	0809	1
spring green	471	255	1502	1
peacock blue	517	169	1107	1
medium mole	642*	392	1906	1
warm cream	677	886	2207	1
faded rose	778	1016	0808	1
old gold	832	907	2202	1
deep blue green	924	851	1706	1
dark sea mist	926	850	1707	1
sea mist	928	274	1708	1
dark forest green	935	861	1507	1
forest green	937	269	1504	1
medium forest green	988	257	1401	1
dark moss green	3011	924	1607	1
dark birch green	3051	268	1508	2
birch green	3052*	859	1509	1
green	3345	263	1507	1
pink	3354	74	0606	1
dark apple green	3362	263	1601	2
deep plum pink	3726	1018	0810	2
bright pink	3731	77	0610	1
dark grape	3740	873	0806	1
medium gray grape	3041	871	0806	2
light gray grape	3042	870	0807	1
medium blue green	3768	851	1706	1
beaver brown	3781	1050	2003	1
murky green	3787	393	1811	1
deep gold	3820	306	2203	1
yellow	3822	305	0109	1
deep plum	3802	1019	0601	1

*colours used extensively in the self coloured embroidery sections

Work with lengths of thread no longer than 18 - 20". If you have the thread any longer in length it will become rubbed and weakened.

Needles
The needle, the embroidery thread and the thread of the fabric to be embroidered should be of the same thickness. A tapestry needle is best to work with as it does not split the threads of the fabric you are embroidering. The size of needle to use with the different counts of linen are -

Threads per inch	Tapestry needle size
28	24
30 - 32	26
35	28

Scissors
A pair of small sharp pointed scissors, kept purely for cutting threads, is required.

Frames
A small round wooden frame is best for using with this embroidery. I recommend one from 10 cm (4 ") to 18 cm (7 "). My personal favourite is 15 cm or 6" across the inner ring. Do wrap the inner ring with bias binding to soften the strain on the material while it is being held in the frame. Do not have the frame 'drum tight' or so tight that it marks the linen or stitching. I 'sew stitch' all cross stitch. (For more information on 'sew stitch' please refer to page 16.)

Laying Tool
A laying tool ensures that your threads lie flat, side by side so that the sheen on the threads reflects the maximum light. I find using a laying tool with a slight 'bulb' at the end particularly helpful as the threads stay in position and do not slip off the tool until I am ready.

Stiletto
A tool that every embroiderer needs! A stiletto needs to sharp enough to be able to pierce closely woven linen and smooth enough to be used in pulled thread embroidery where I use it to make perfect eyelets every time. (See circular eyelet p21.)

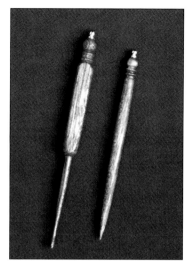

Laying Tool and Stiletto (note slight "bulb" at the tip of the laying tool.

Stitching Techniques

Before you Begin

All even weave linen will fray easily when handled. To avoid this oversew all raw edges before starting your embroidery. Use a fine sewing machine thread matching the colour of the linen so that the edging can be left on when the hem is turned in. If a heavy thread is used it may show through the hem or cause an uneven ridge. Use a three stitch zig zag, serpentine stitch or whatever variation your machine has which does not have long stitches as these may shrink and pull when your masterpiece is given a wash.

Sewing Methods

There are two different methods of sewing the different stitches in this sampler.

Stab Stitch - in this method of sewing there are two movements - the needle is taken from the front to the back in one movement and then from the back to the front in a second separate movement. This method is more generally used for work in large frames, canvas, tapestry, some parts of gold work, stump work and crewel work but is also used by some for satin and cross stitch.

Sew Stitch - this is my favoured method of sewing cross and satin stitches. It is ideal to use when work does not have to be held very tightly in a frame. A 'rounder' stitch is formed and it is also a lot quicker as the needle is taken from the back to the front in one movement rather than the two used in 'stab' stitch, see satin stitch in Fig 2.

How to Start

There are a number of different ways of starting your thread. I personally favour leaving a 2 - 3 cm length of thread which I hold under my stitching, catching it in as I go.

Surface method - If you are a beginner you may find it easier to leave a length of thread on the surface of the material to be finished later. To do this take your needle from the front to the back of the work, approximately 5 cm away from where you plan to start stitching, leaving a 5 cm length of thread on top of the fabric. Start to stitch and when you have covered some distance the thread on top of your work is taken to the back and finished into your stitching. (Fig 1)

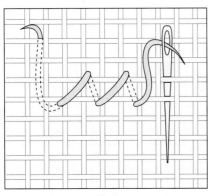

Fig 1

Back Stitch - When you are working satin stitch you can work a couple of little back stitches in an area that will later be covered by the satin stitch.

Long Thread Method - Another handy tip is to use an extra long thread. Start stitching with half the length of thread, use up all the thread working one way, then rethread your needle with the remaining length of thread, turn your work around and work in the other direction. This is particularly useful for satin stitch and the stems in cross stitch designs. (Fig 2)

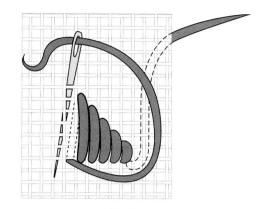

Fig 2

Loop Method – Very useful when you are using a double thread. Take one long length of thread, fold in half and thread the cut ends through the eye of the needle. Start stitching in the correct position as shown on the chart, taking the needle under one thread, then thread the needle through the loop, now stitch the design following the chart. Neat and quick without a knot in sight! (Fig 3)

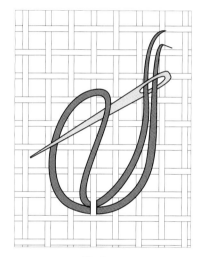

Fig 3

Finishing

At the back of your work take the needle under your stitching for about 2 cms (3/4 of an inch), do a little slip or half knot then thread the needle back the 2 cms and cut.

Whip the thread end up a row of stitches rather than across for a tidier finish in cross stitch. (fig 4)

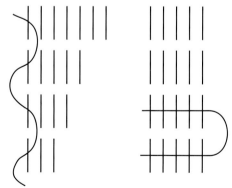

Fig 4

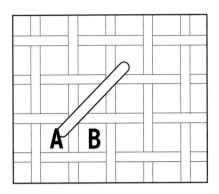

Fig 1

Cross Stitch

Cross stitch was known to the ancient Egyptians and was such an important part of everyday lives that embroidery frames were put into the tombs of aristocratic ladies. Cross Stitch patterns can be found in most of the different cultures of the world from Egypt and Iran to the Balkans and in countries throughout Europe. It is found decorating christening shawls, cradle covers, on trousseau bed linen, altar cloths and clerical robes.

Where to Start Stitching
Start where a vertical thread is lying on top of the horizontal thread, marked A, see fig. 1

With the first stitch starting where a vertical thread is lying on top of the horizontal thread, as shown, all following stitches will start in the same position throughout your embroidery. As well as making a neater stitch it is a most useful check. If you come to start a new stitch and it is beside a horizontal thread (marked B) you instantly know that somewhere you have sewn over one or three threads, not two. Check as you sew and also at the start of the return row when working a long line of stitches.

Stitching Hints

- Always neaten fabric edges before you begin to stitch.

- Use the right size needle for the work.

- When moving the needle down the thread always place the thread in the centre of the eye of the needle so there is less 'drag' on the thread.

- Do not fold your work, roll it round a tube encased in acid free tissue.

- Never leave the needle in the fabric, in time it may rust, leaving a most unattractive and unwanted stain.

- Do not leave the work rolled up on a frame for any length of time - loosen the roller or hoop until you are ready to start working again.

- When stitching an alphabet, always end the thread after each letter is completed.

- When pressing your work put a folded tablecloth on the table and lay your embroidery face down on the tablecloth before pressing. The tablecloth has a little 'give' which prevents your embroidery being completely flattened! If you do by chance 'flatten' your embroidery with over enthusiastic ironing rinse again in clean water and then iron gently.

Always work the first stitch from left to right and the second stitch right to left, fig. 2. For a professional finish all cross stitches must have the top diagonal thread lying in the same direction.

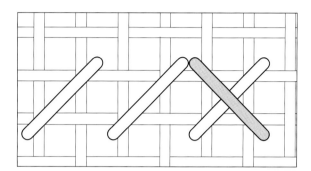

Fig 2

When you are stitching you may find it easier to work in a certain area or follow a particular pattern if you turn your work around. If you have worked the first half of some of your stitches and then decide the angle is not comfortable *turn your work 180 degrees* and you will see the first half of your cross stitch is still lying left to right so that you can happily continue your stitching at the new angle. Do not turn your work 90 or 270 degrees as this will cause irregularities in the way your stitching lies.

How to stitch -

Outside floral borders - Stitch the central stem first and always stitch a length equal to two or three repeats of the pattern before working the flowers, leaves etc. Stitch in one direction working from top to bottom, or whatever is comfortable for you. Turning your work 180⁰ (as mentioned above) may be helpful to ensure the fabric can be held comfortably in your hands.

The inside bands - these small bands are worked right across the space from left to right.

Carrying colours - when using two thread colours at once have a needle with each coloured thread.

Changing threads - to carry your thread from one area to the next - slide the needle through the stitches at the back.

Turning corners - complete the last stitch on one side before turning your work and beginning a new line of stitching.

18 x 50cm
Band Sampler worked entirely
in cross stitch.

Self Coloured Embroidery

In self coloured embroidery the texture of the stitching is the most important feature. It is usually worked in shades of one colour.

The stitches and techniques shown here feature in the two central side sections of my sampler and were inspired by the pulled and drawn thread work often referred to as 'white work' found in seventeenth century Band Samplers. Some of the band samplers were entirely made up of white work designs, others featured this embroidery just across the base of the sampler.

Counted Satin Stitch

(also known as Geometric satin stitch)

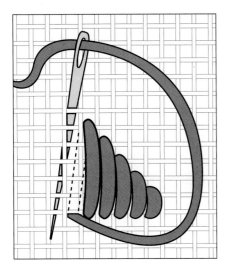

This is a stitch with lots of possibilities! The basic satin stitch dates back to ancient times and many variations of the stitch have developed over the centuries. The stitch may be left flat against the fabric or pulled tight depending on the effect required. It may be worked in blocks or to create a pattern.

The stitches should lie adjacent to each other without overlapping. The thread should be kept evenly twisted throughout the work by turning the needle in the fingers when necessary. Each stitch should lie flat on the fabric and should not 'pull' the threads out of position. It is stitched using a tapestry needle.

A laying tool can be useful when working satin stitch to achieve a really smooth finished stitch. Satin stitch may be worked in either the 'stab' stitch or 'sew stitch' method. For more information on these two methods of sewing see page 16.

To Start
Satin stitch is usually worked in blocks and this makes it very easy to start - just work a couple of little back stitches in an area that will later be covered by the satin stitch or use the Loop Method (page 17.)

To Finish
Take your needle through to the back of your work, slip it under the stitching for a short distance, do a little slip knot and then take the needle under the stitching for a further distance.

Holbein Stitch

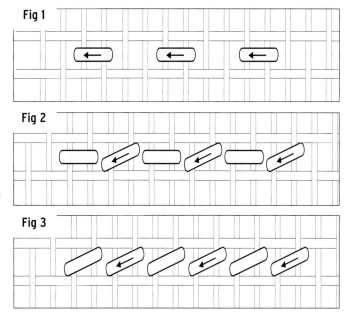

Fig 1

Fig 2

Fig 3

Holbein stitch is worked in running stitch in two journeys using a tapestry needle. It is important to keep the thread tension even. In the first journey the stitches are evenly spaced leaving gaps to be filled in on the return journey (fig. 1).

There are different methods you can choose for working the return journey and the method I find most satisfactory is to bring my needle up through the fabric above the thread of the first journey and then go down below it, (fig. 2).

After adjusting the thread tension your stitches will line up as shown (fig. 3).

Eyelets

Eyelets give an attractive contrast to satin stitch. The tension of the stitching must be firm so the holes in the eyelets are all the same size. Bring the needle (tapestry) up in the outer edge and take it down through the centre for all variations of this stitch. This enables you to pull the thread away from the centre. Work around each eyelet in the sequence given.

Square Eyelet
Always start at the outside of the eyelet and take the needle down in the centre. Work around in sequence following the diagram (fig. 1). I find it easier to start in the corner.

Circular Eyelet
To create a nice shape, give a gentle push with a stiletto into the centre to start the eyelet but do not make the hole so big that the thread count is lost. Note *there are no stitches on the straight* in this eyelet. On completion, another gentle push with the stiletto rounds it nicely and 'sets' the stitching. This gives a lovely circular eyelet with a fine edge. (fig 2)

To start all single eyelets hold the thread with a finger on the wrong side under the stitching and catch it in as you move around - a knack soon acquired when stitching lots of these! Each eyelet is complete in itself.

All even numbers are in the centre

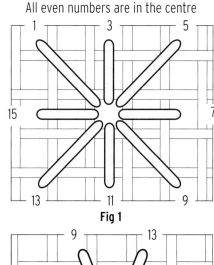

Fig 1

All even numbers are in the centre
Fig 2

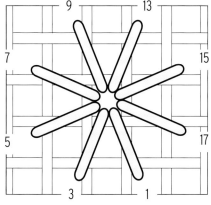

To finish at the back of the work thread the needle under the worked stitches and cut thread.

If it is being worked in a border or close to other stitching the thread may be carried from one to the next by slipping the thread under the stitches at the back of the work.

Antique Hem Stitch

This hem stitch is used to secure the hem of the sampler. Stitch using a fine tapestry needle to avoid splitting the threads.
This stitch is worked from left to right. Hold your work with the folded edge of the hem against your body and the hem facing you.

Bring the needle up two threads down from the folded edge of the hem, take the needle to the right pass it behind four threads of fabric at the edge of the hem (fig. 1). Next take the needle between the fabric and the hem (beside your first stitch) bring it through the hem two threads down as before (fig. 2). Continue in this way.

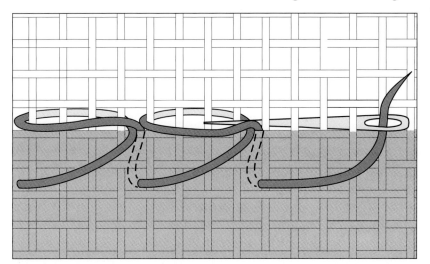

Fig 1

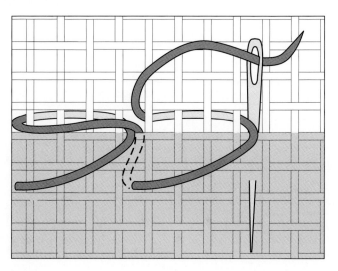

Fig 2

Ribbon stitch

This is another stitch with various names. I prefer its Danish name - Ribbon Stitch to the alternative Reversed Faggot Stitch. This is a stitch that is always worked on the diagonal, it can be worked over two or three threads as required.

It is a row of three stitches worked on the diagonal. Each row of three stitches is worked at once then the needle is brought up at the top of the worked stitches to work the second row.
To learn, ribbon stitch is shown worked over two threads.

Row 1
Bring your thread through where indicated and work two diagonal stitches as shown taking your needle up and along two threads with each stitch, then take your needle down in the correct position to complete the third diagonal stitch (up and along two threads) but bring it out at the *top* of the first worked stitch (fig. 1).
The second row is worked on top of the first row of worked stitches in the same way. When working the third diagonal stitch bring the needle out at the top of the first stitch worked in this row. (fig 2)

Repeat these rows until you are four threads from the highest point you wish to reach. (If working over three threads it would of course be six threads from the highest point.)

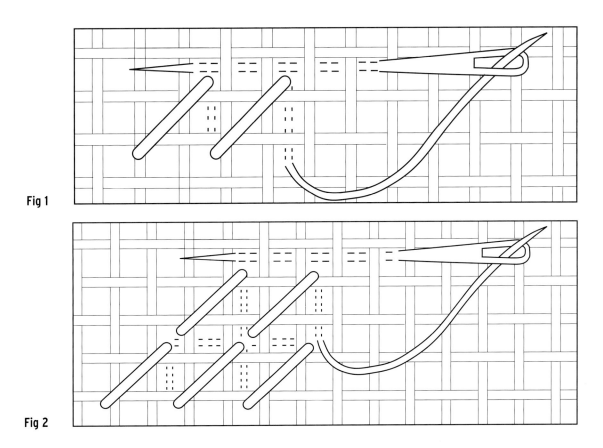

Fig 1

Fig 2

To turn take your needle to the correct position for starting the next row but only work the first *two* stitches before taking your needle back to the usual starting position for a new row, fig 3.

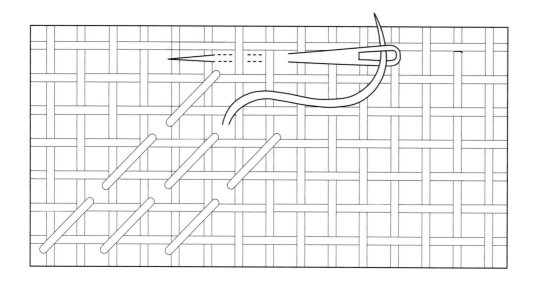

Fig 3

Now work *one* stitch only, fig. 4.

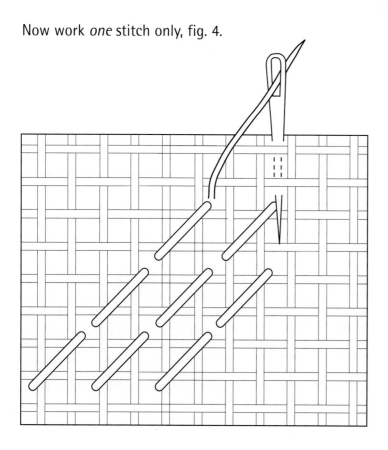

Fig 4

Next take the needle down and to the right two threads but bring the needle out at the top, fig. 5.

Fig 5

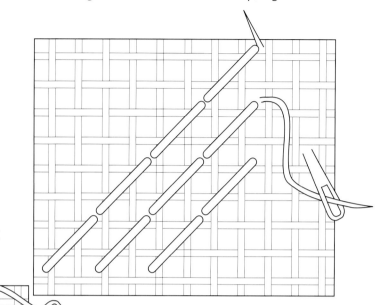

Take the needle down, two threads down and to the right and bring it to the front at the top of the lower row of stitches, fig. 6.

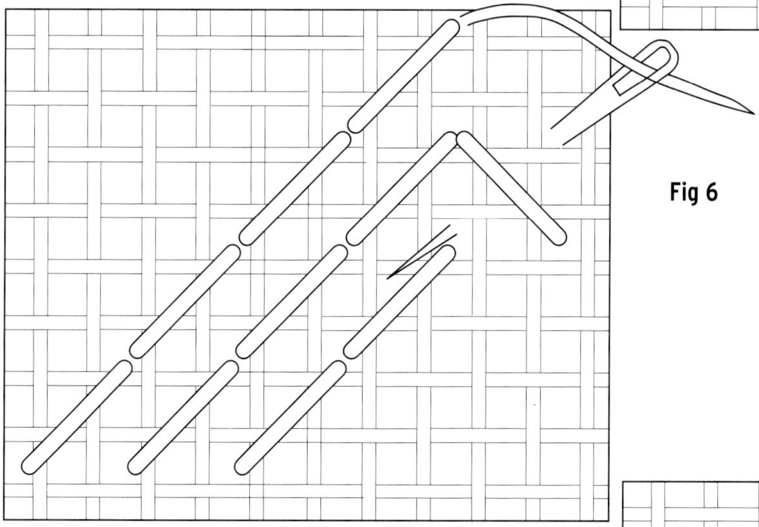

Fig 6

Work one further stitch taking the needle to the back, two threads down and to the right, but coming to the front at the right hand lower end of the top stitch, fig. 7. Turn your work round 90 degrees and continue in the manner described in Row 1, fig. 1

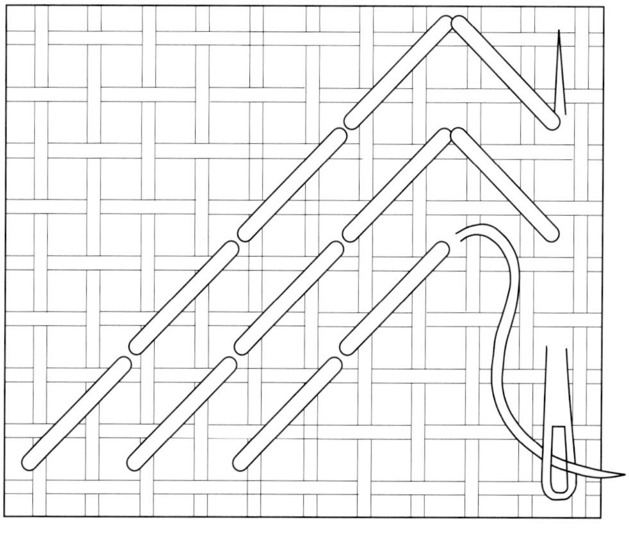

Fig 7

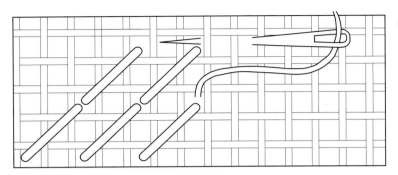

Fig 8

To work a left hand turn follow
figures 8, 9, 10 and 11.

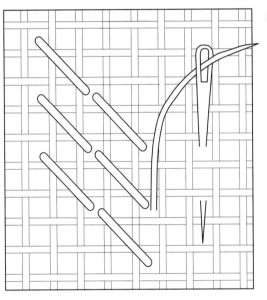

Fig 9

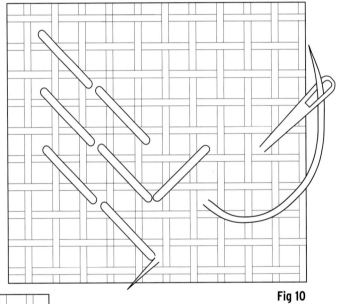

Fig 10

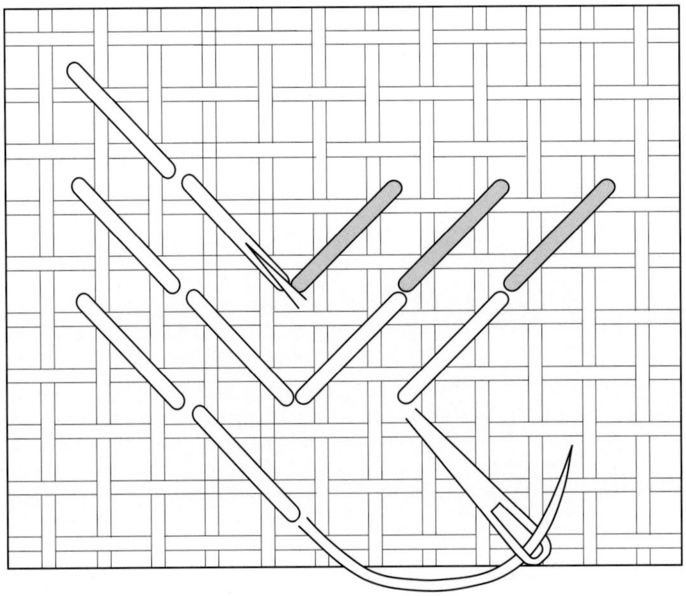

Shaded stitches inidcate first complete
row to be worked in new direction

Fig 11

Filet Embroidery

Originally this embroidery was worked on net with a square mesh. It was constructed with a special needle and gauge to ensure all the mesh squares were the same size - a fishing net was the first knotted mesh in use. Now we make a mesh out of material.

When referring to the chart for filet darning <u>each square equals two threads and each line between equals two threads</u>. This forms the foundation for the stitching.

To Start

Tack over and under two threads right across the area this embroidery is to be worked in. From the satin stitch border on the left, to the satin stitch border on the right, leaving a tail of thread at each end.

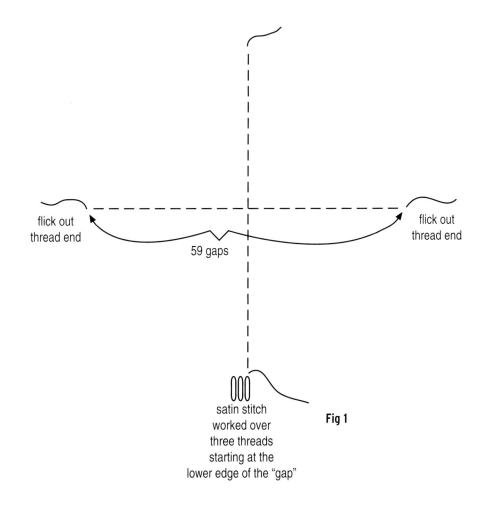

flick out thread end

59 gaps

flick out thread end

satin stitch worked over three threads starting at the lower edge of the "gap"

Fig 1

The partner to the whitework Sampler featured on page 6. This Sampler has extensive filet embroidery panels.

When tacking the vertical line start at the centre with the first stitch coming from the same hole as the horizontal line of tacking. Tack over and under two threads, fig. 1 Tack down to the zig zag satin stitch at the base of the design area then rethread your needle and tack up from the centre covering a distance greater than the size of the design panel, again leaving a tail of thread at each end.

Count 59 gaps (both panels are the same width) across the design area and flick out the thread at each end.

A Gap = threads showing between tacked stitches. See illustrations on pages 27 and 29.

Block 4 band 6 count 16 gaps vertically and flick out each end of thread. **Block 6 band 6** count 15 gaps vertically and flick out each end of thread.

Using one thread of coton a broder 16 work satin stitch over three threads around the entire design area, starting at the lower edge of the 'gap'. Work one diagonal stitch in the corner as shown.

To cut and remove the threads is simple. Work round the rectangle in the order given on the illustration, always cutting the threads close to the satin stitching.

With these edge threads removed you will find it is much easier to cut and remove the rest of the threads. Work along one side of the satin stitch at the inner edge of the design area and cut and remove every alternate two threads along this edge. Cut two threads then pull them out back to the satin stitch edge on the opposite side then cut right up against the satin stitching. When you have removed every alternate two threads in one direction, repeat in the other direction.

Your work area is now outlined with satin stitch and every two alternate threads have been withdrawn back to the satin stitch and cut off.

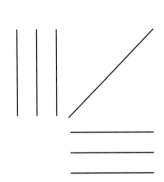

Handy Hint
Should you cut a thread by mistake - don't panic, take a thread of the material from close to the edge and weave it in to replace the cut thread, finish it neatly on the back of your Sampler in the satin stitching.

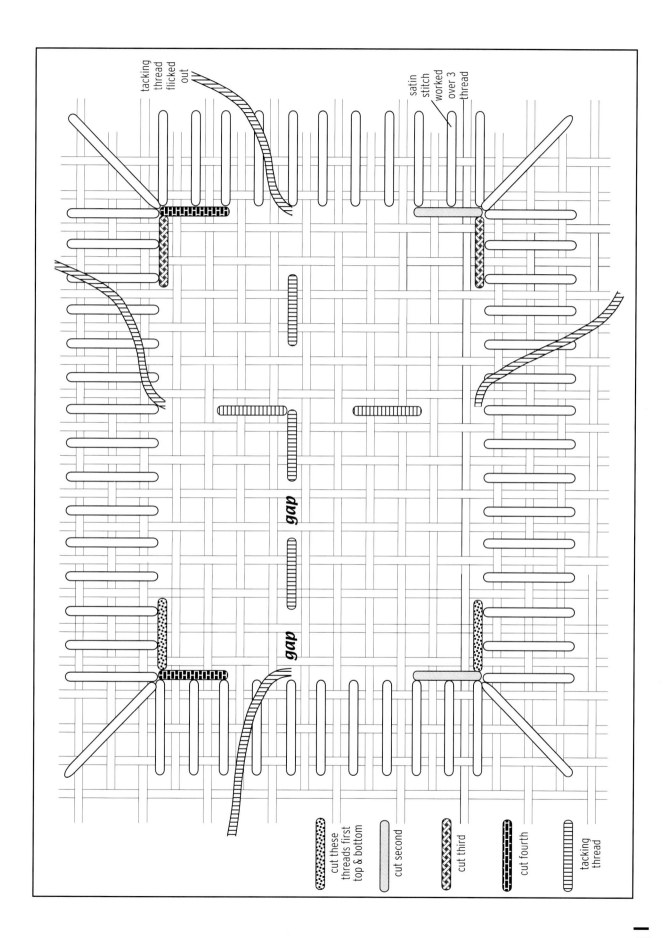

tacking thread flicked out

satin stitch worked over 3 thread

gap

gap

cut these threads first top & bottom

cut second

cut third

cut fourth

tacking thread

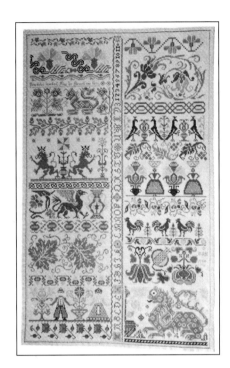

42 x 65cm
Double Band Sampler worked by the
author in the style of a mid-late 17th
Century English Sampler in the
Fitzwilliam Museum

The two separate threads are now whipped together to form a single heavier 'bar'. Whip all horizontal rows first. To do this, four intersections down from the satin stitch edging, run a thread up the middle of the two threads to the satin stitch, slide the thread through the satin stitching on the back of the work to further anchor the thread before bringing the needle out to the left of the bar. Wrap the thread around the bar twice in each opening see fig. 4. All whipping stitches are worked from left to right.

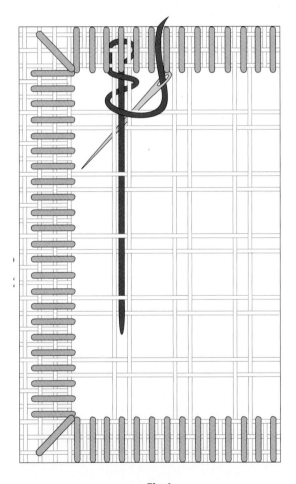

Fig 4

When you have completed the first bar, take your thread into the back of the satin stitching to anchor it before whipping the next two threads to form a bar in the same way. Always turn your work 180^0 so that you are working down the design area. Repeat until all bars have been whipped, (fig. 5).

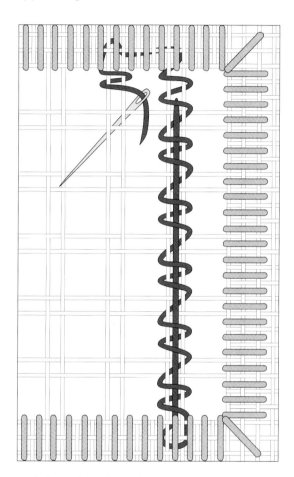

Fig 5

If you run out of thread in the middle of a bar, finish the old thread by running it down the centre of the threads that have not yet been whipped - this will be anchored when you continue stitching. Start the new thread by anchoring it in the satin stitch and running it down the whipped bar to the correct starting position. This avoids excess bulk at any one point.

The vertical bars are worked in the same manner. Turn your work around so that you always work from the top down.
In this embroidery I have whipped the bars with a fine thread and stitched the design using a heavier thread so in this instance it is not possible to work the Ghost stitch design whilst whipping the bars.
The threads to be used are given with each design. See pages 69 and 79.

Ghost Stitch

To start
Run your needle up through the whipped threads at the back of your work until you reach the starting position

To work individual stitches
Work individual stitches following the diagrams - a buttonhole stitch is worked at the top, right and lower sides with the needle being taken down to the right of the starting thread to complete the stitch. Move to the starting position for the next stitch by running your needle through the whipping threads at the back of your work.

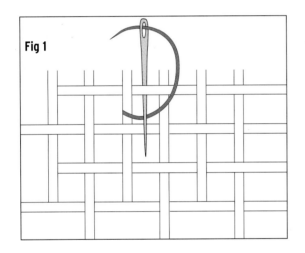

Fig 1

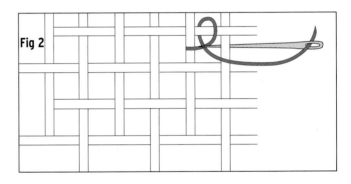

Fig 2

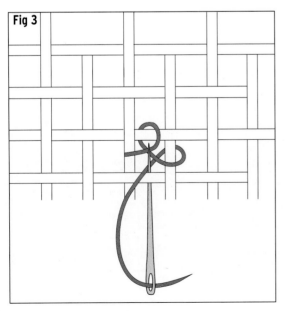

Fig 3

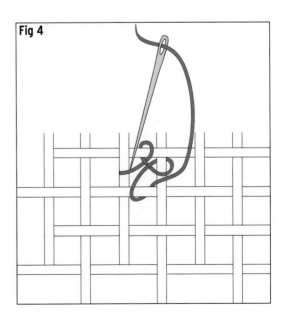

Fig 4

To work in rows

Referring to the diagrams, bring your needle to the front at the centre left of the bar and work buttonhole stitches loosely along the row, (fig. 1). The loops should be more than half way down the 'square' they are filling. Hold the loops down with your thumb as you are stitching to ensure they do not pull up.

At the end of the row work one stitch at the right hand edge of the row before working back completing each stitch.

On the return row a buttonhole stitch is worked at the base of each square, then the needle must be taken over the loop and under the bar as shown fig. 2.

Continue working in this way to finish the row. The last stitch is completed by taking the needle down to the right of the starting thread and anchoring in the whipping.

Fig 1

Fig 2

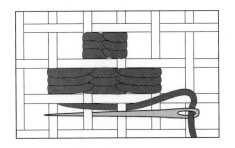

Needleweave Filling

To start run the thread up through the whipping at the back of the design panel bringing your needle out left of the bar at the top of the square you wish to fill with needleweaving.

Go over and under the bars until the required area has been filled.

How to stitch a perfect Mitred Corner Everytime!

To stitch a perfect mitred corner the time spent in preparation is essential. Decide where your hem is to fold into, this is the inside edge of the hem and the first line of tacking must go here - the solid line in the diagram fig.1.

Decide on the width of the hem, ours is 1 cm (1/2") wide so all lines are tacked 1 cm apart. (You may prefer to count the number of threads in 1cm and count threads rather than measure.)

Tack a second line - the long dashed line - 1 cm from the inner line of tacking.
Tack a third line - the dotted line - 1 cm from the second line of tacking. Trim your fabric back so that the material extending beyond the third line of tacking is slightly less than the width of the hem, fig. 1. Fold the shaded area in, at the corners fold one side on top of the other and tack in place fig 2.

Fig 1

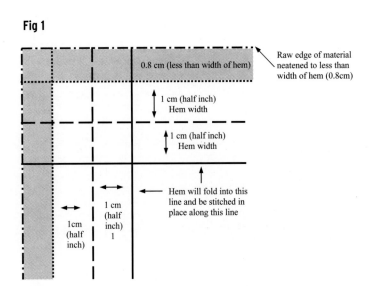

0.8 cm (less than width of hem)

Raw edge of material neatened to less than width of hem (0.8cm)

1 cm (half inch) Hem width

1 cm (half inch) Hem width

Hem will fold into this line and be stitched in place along this line

1cm (half inch)

1 cm (half inch) 1

Fig 2

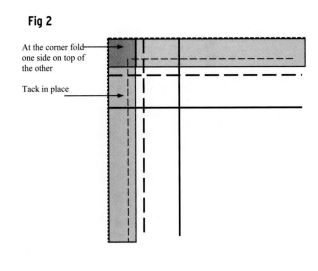

At the corner fold one side on top of the other

Tack in place

Now fold each corner down to the inner tacked corner, tack across the diagonal to hold fabric in place and cut the shaded area off, fig. 3.

Pick up the fabric and fold the corner between the finger and thumb, pinching it together tightly so that points 'A' and 'B' are together. Using fine thread oversew the corner together, starting where indicated. At the edge put your finger inside to ensure the fabric is spread flat and then lay the mitred corner against the inner line of tacking and work two or three stitches at the corner to hold it exactly in position. Stitch all four mitred corners before hemming the sides.

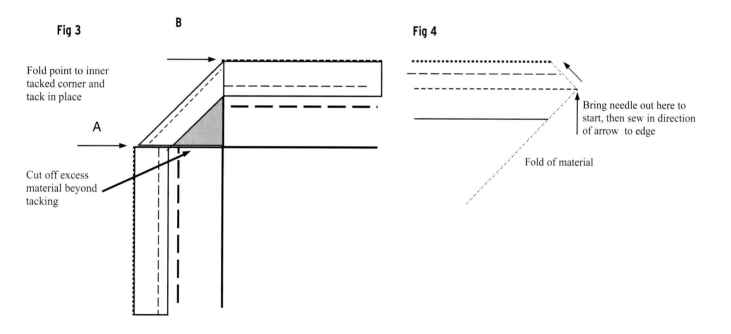

Fig 3

B

Fold point to inner tacked corner and tack in place

A

Cut off excess material beyond tacking

Fig 4

Bring needle out here to start, then sew in direction of arrow to edge

Fold of material

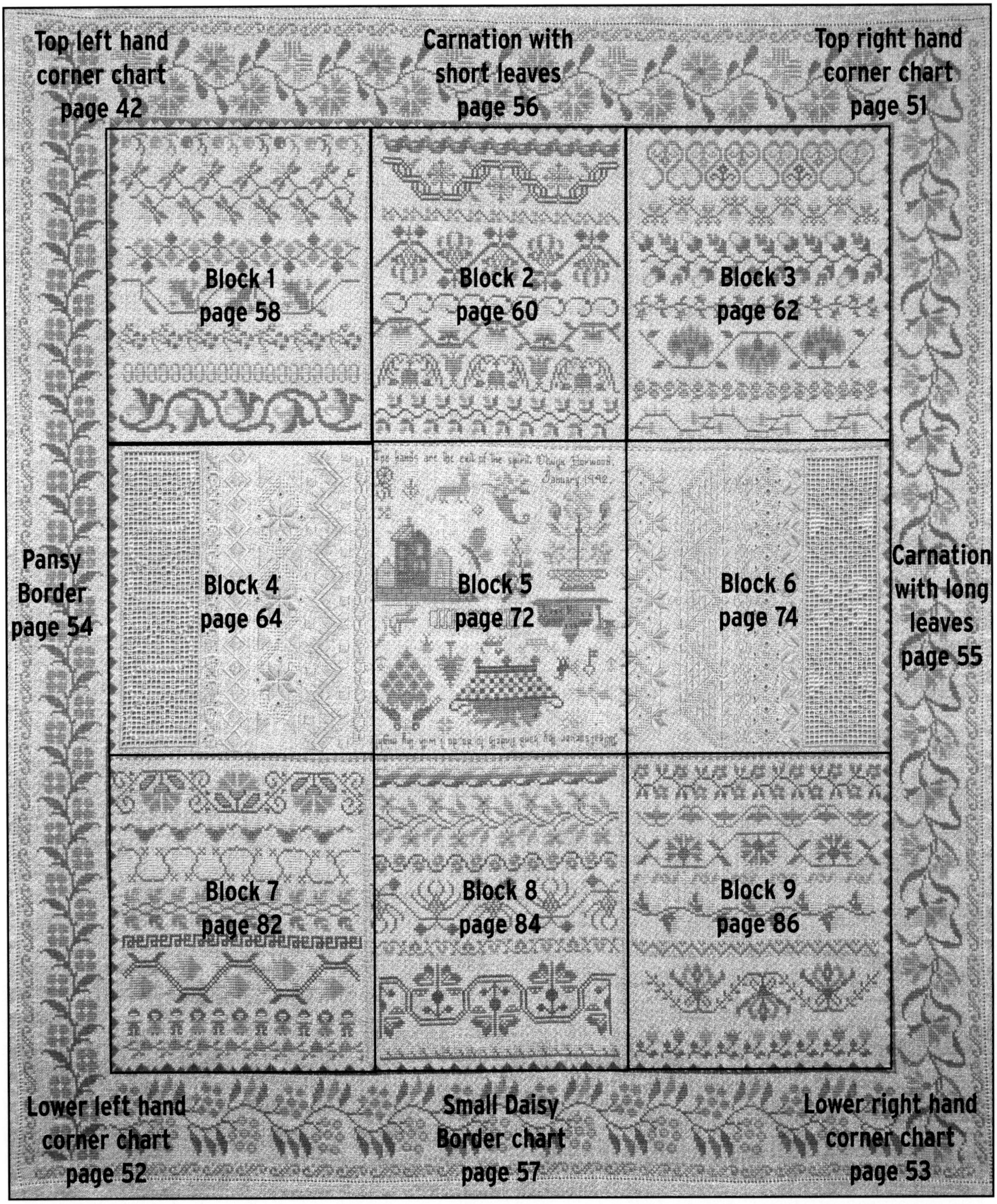

Top left hand
corner chart
page 42

Carnation with
short leaves
page 56

Top right hand
corner chart
page 51

Block 1
page 58

Block 2
page 60

Block 3
page 62

Pansy
Border
page 54

Block 4
page 64

Block 5
page 72

Block 6
page 74

Carnation
with long
leaves
page 55

Block 7
page 82

Block 8
page 84

Block 9
page 86

Lower left hand
corner chart
page 52

Small Daisy
Border chart
page 57

Lower right hand
corner chart
page 53

How To Stitch

Once Upon A Band

These instructions are for stitching Once Upon a Band using linen with 28 - 35 threads per inch. The same instructions apply to the different weights of linen.

Starting the Design
Neaten the raw edges of the linen by hand or machine, see Before you Begin page 16.

This sampler can be viewed from any angle, however for easy reference I have arbitrarily assigned a 'top' and 'bottom' to the design. The entire sampler is shown on the front cover and in chart form on the facing page with the different sections identified for reference.

This is a large Sampler and I feel it is easier to start at the top left hand corner of the design. Measure in 10 cm (4") from the top and left hand sides and start with the small repeating border found right round the outside of the Sampler. Work in from this point stitching the two large floral borders down each side next as they line up with the small outside repeating border and are worked from top to bottom. The large floral borders across the top and bottom are worked next as these fit in between the two side floral borders. I worked the entire border design before stitching the satin stitch saw tooth design and then the nine inner blocks. I would advise leaving the self coloured embroidery until last.

The Charts
All charts overlap so that it is easy to move from one chart to the next.

Corners
The corner designs are given separately in charts which show a small portion of the large floral borders as they are stitched in each corner - refer to the corner charts before you start stitching the large floral borders as some of the corners sections do start and finish mid pattern. The corner charts are shown on pages 42, 51-53.

Four large floral Borders

Each floral border is given separately. Once you have started the large floral border designs in the corners you will need to turn to the border pattern shown in full for the pattern repeat. The 'pansy border' on the left hand side is shown on page 54, the 'carnation with short leaves border' which runs across the top of the Sampler is shown on page 56. The 'carnation with long leaves border' which runs down the right hand side of the Sampler is shown on page 55 and the 'small daisy border' which runs across the base of the Sampler is shown on page 57.

Nine Inner Sections - Blocks 1 - 9

The nine inner sections are each shown in a large, clear double page chart with threads to be used. They are numbered from left to right and top to bottom as shown on the chart. Each block shows the satin stitch borders surrounding it so that placement of the pattern bands is easy.

The positioning of bands is very flexible and the notion of every band being centred is very much a twentieth century idea. I much prefer the more natural seventeenth and eighteenth century approach which was to start stitching and continue until you ran out of space without consideration to whether this was at the start or finish of a pattern or in the middle! This is the way I have positioned my bands on the Sampler, except for the larger bands with three motifs which are centred, as I feel this helps balance the narrower bands.

To Finish - the Hem and Mitred Corners

This sampler has a narrow hem which is held in place with Antique Hem stitch see page 22. The corners are all mitred and to make a perfect mitred corner every time refer to page 34.

The Stitches

The main borders and blocks are stitched in cross stitch. Refer to page 18 for expert advice on working perfect cross stitch!

The borders are separated from the inner nine blocks by a saw tooth satin stitch design and the inner nine blocks are each separated by further satin stitch borders.

The self coloured pattern bands in Blocks 4 & 6 are a combination of satin and ribbon stitches along with circular and square eyelets. These are enjoyable to stitch and a little different. All the stitches used are shown on pages 18 - 35 in large clear, easy to follow diagrams. If you don't already know these stitches with our clear instructions you will enjoy learning them!

Band 6 of Blocks 4 & 6 is worked in filet embroidery. Excellent illustrations of this different technique are given on pages 27- 34. These small panels are an enjoyable way of learning this attractive technique. We also give alternative satin stitch bands that could be used in these areas on pages 70 - 71 design for Block 4 and Pages 80 - 81 design for Block 6. Choose the designs you prefer.

Threads for cross stitch

I recommend using one thread of stranded cotton for all cross stitch when working on linen with 28 - 35 threads to the inch. One thread of stranded cotton gives a fine antique look to the sampler but if you feel you would like a heavier look work a test sample on the edge of the linen using two threads of stranded cotton and then beside it work a test block using one thread of stranded cotton. Choose the stitching with the effect you find most pleasing.

Threads for self coloured embroidery in blocks 4 & 6

The weight of thread to use when working the various stitches on different linen counts is given here. Detailed instructions for the colours and threads to use are given with the stitch instructions for each band.

Stitches	28 threads per inch	30 threads per inch	32 threads per inch	35 threads per inch
Back stitch	One thread of stranded cotton			
Holbein stitch	One thread of coton a broder 25		One thread of stranded cotton	
Ribbon stitch	16 or 25 coton a broder, follow instructions in embroidery, the same thread is used on all linens			
Counted satin stitch	Two threads of stranded cotton		One thread of stranded cotton	
Satin stitch edging around filet embroidery	Coton a broder 16			
Whipping	One thread of stranded cotton			
Ghost stitch	Coton a broder 25			
Needle weaving	Coton a broder 16			

How To Stitch

Once Upon A Band As A Small Sampler

Using One Block

- One block of Once Upon a Band could be stitched most effectively creating a small rectangular sampler.

- You could stitch one block and add a narrow border pattern round it selected from another area of Once Upon a Band. Drop one band pattern and insert a verse and your name and date in the space.

- Alternatively you could select band patterns related to a particular flower e.g. carnations, or fruit e.g. the strawberry - a very popular embroidery subject in the seventeenth century.

- You could work your sampler on a theme choosing just white work.

Using two blocks

- Stitch two blocks of Once Upon a Band to make a longer narrow sampler. Choose band patterns from the coloured thread and self colour sections to create a Sampler reminiscent of the seventeenth century English Samplers which combined colour with white work.

- Do something a little different. Start with the alphabet at the top worked in two or three colours of the same shade then select a wide band pattern to have at the base to give definition and balance to your Sampler. Then choose different patterns, wide and narrow, to fill in the space between.

- To achieve a pleasing layout in a Long Narrow Band Sampler I find it is helpful to divide the length of the Sampler into thirds, with different design themes in each area, for example you could have alphabets at the top, coloured bands in the centre and white work at the base. Alternate wide and narrow bands when selecting designs as this gives a more harmonious finished appearance.

Sizing

Theoretically a band sampler is three times as long as it is wide i.e. if your sampler is to be 10 cm (4") wide it should be 30 cm (12") long but in saying that I also hasten to add there are no hard and fast rules so be guided by your own taste and instinct in creating your Sampler.

Repeating Patterns

In placing your bands, to achieve a more traditional look don't centre the designs, rather start the band at the left hand edge and just stitch until you run out of space - as early needlewomen did! If you prefer to centre a design, and this is a matter of personal preference, count the number of stitches in a pattern, for example if there are 20 stitches in one pattern and there is a space of 105 stitches, the band will fit five times with five stitches left over. Work two extra stitches at one end and three at the other.

In this book I give you a large selection of some of the band patterns I have admired and collected over the years. Add to it to create your own reference library of patterns. Keep a folder especially for the purpose and keep alphabets, band patterns and pictures of layouts that appeal, also refer to the Sampler Books listed in the Reference Section for a wealth of ideas and inspiration.

Fabric Required

To work out the amount of fabric required to stitch a sampler count the width of the pattern (e.g. the width of Block 1 is 110 squares). Each square of the chart represents two threads so if the block width is 110 squares multiply by 2 for the number of threads = 220 threads. To work out the length of fabric required repeat this process.

The number of threads per inch in the fabric you choose to work with will determine the width of fabric you need to buy. Divide the number of threads in the design e.g. 220 by the thread count in the fabric you wish to use e.g. 28 threads per inch.

220 ÷ 28 = 7 3/4 inches add 4 inches for edges so you need to buy a piece of fabric approximately 12 inches wide by the length you have decided on.

220 ÷ 30 = 7 1/4 inches
220 ÷ 32 = 6 3/4 inches
220 ÷ 35 = 6 1/4 inches

Start your Sampler and choose the band patterns as you work, you will find it a most satisfying and enjoyable experience!

15 x 43cm
A variety of acorn and oak leaf patterns were stitched in autumn tones for the authors son.

Corner Charts

Start Here

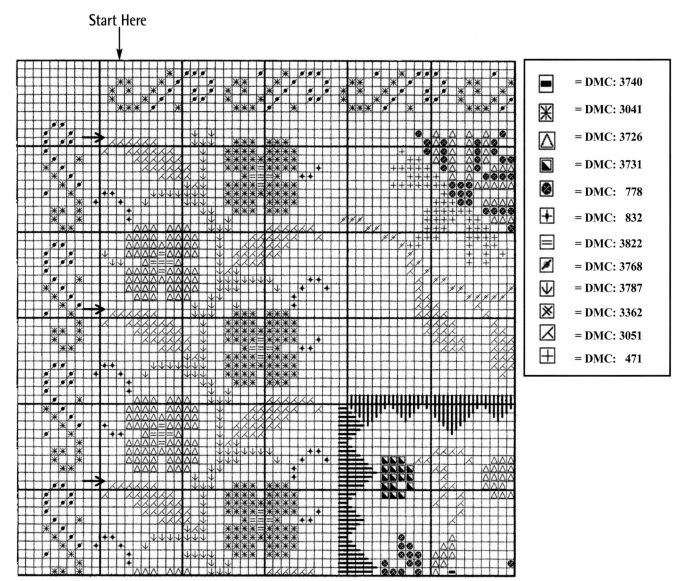

	= DMC: 3740
	= DMC: 3041
	= DMC: 3726
	= DMC: 3731
	= DMC: 778
	= DMC: 832
	= DMC: 3822
	= DMC: 3768
	= DMC: 3787
	= DMC: 3362
	= DMC: 3051
	= DMC: 471

<u>Each square on this chart represents two threads of fabric</u>
tpi = threads per inch
Refer to the frontispiece for additional detail

All cross stitch is worked using one thread of stranded cotton. For additional information on this refer to page 39.

The saw tooth satin stitch is worked using 1 thread of stranded cotton 3362 for linen with a thread count of 31 - 35tpi, 2 threads for 28 - 30tpi.

Blocks 4-6 Centre

Alternative satin stitch
design provided see
pages 70-71

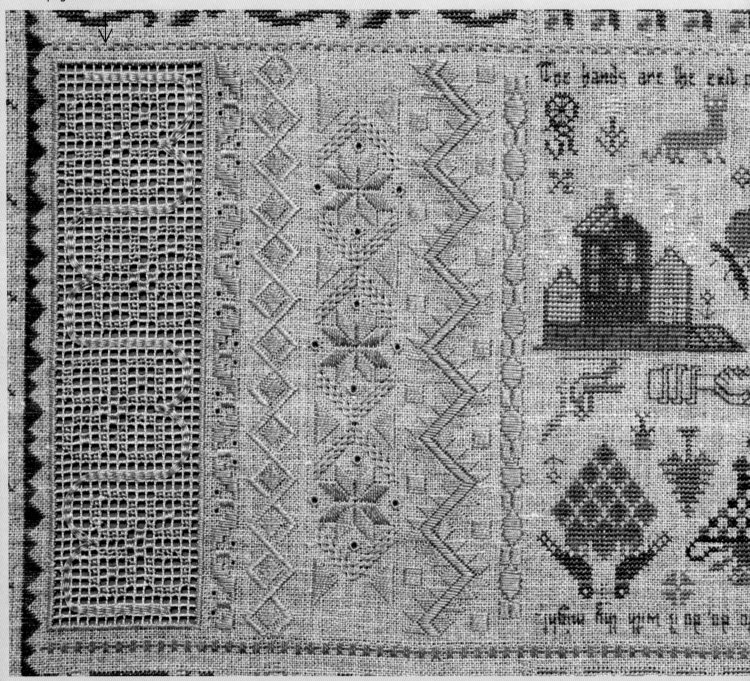

Alternative satin stitch
design provided see
pages 80-81

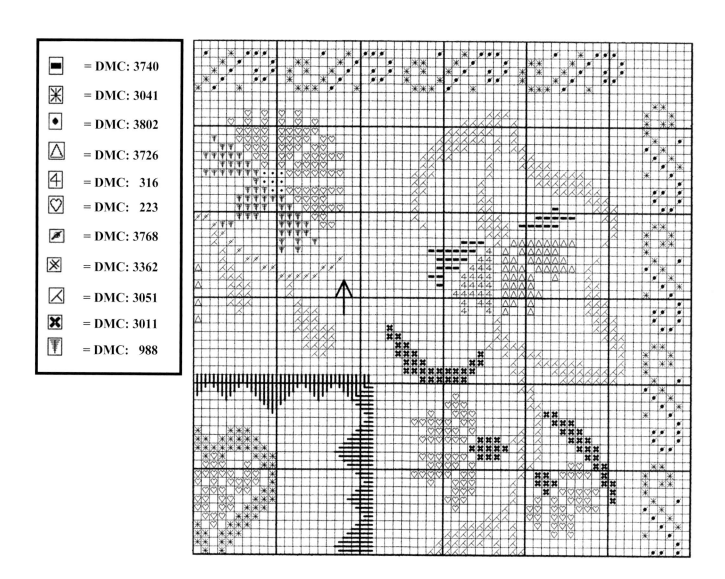

◼	= DMC: 3740
米	= DMC: 3041
◆	= DMC: 3802
△	= DMC: 3726
4	= DMC: 316
♡	= DMC: 223
✐	= DMC: 3768
⊠	= DMC: 3362
◿	= DMC: 3051
✖	= DMC: 3011
⊤	= DMC: 988

Chart Top Right Hand Corner

<u>Each square on this chart represents two threads of fabric</u>
tpi = threads per inch
Refer to the frontispiece for additional detail

All cross stitch is worked using one thread of stranded cotton. For additional information on this refer to page 39.

The saw tooth satin stitch is worked using 1 thread of stranded cotton 3362 for linen with a thread count of 31 - 35tpi, 2 threads for 28 - 30tpi.

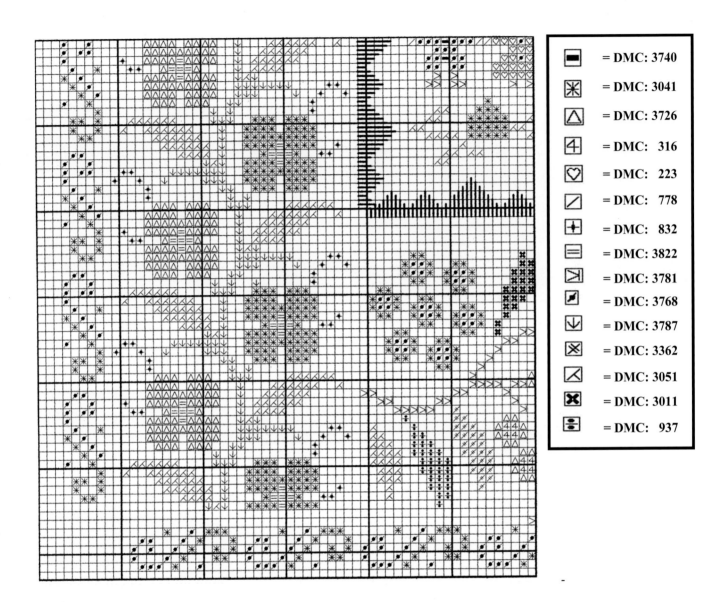

⬛	= DMC: 3740
✳	= DMC: 3041
△	= DMC: 3726
4	= DMC: 316
♡	= DMC: 223
⧄	= DMC: 778
⊞	= DMC: 832
⊟	= DMC: 3822
⊵	= DMC: 3781
⬕	= DMC: 3768
↓	= DMC: 3787
⊠	= DMC: 3362
⬕	= DMC: 3051
✖	= DMC: 3011
⬌	= DMC: 937

Chart Lower Left Hand Corner

<u>Each square on this chart represents two threads of fabric</u>

tpi = threads per inch

Refer to the frontispiece for additional detail

All cross stitch is worked using one thread of stranded cotton. For additional information on this refer to page 39.

The saw tooth satin stitch is worked using 1 thread of stranded cotton 3362 for linen with a thread count of 31 - 35tpi, 2 threads for 28 - 30tpi.

▬	= DMC: 3740
✳	= DMC: 3041
△	= DMC: 3726
4	= DMC: 316
♡	= DMC: 223
◣	= DMC: 3731
◉	= DMC: 3787
✎	= DMC: 3768
✗	= DMC: 3362
◺	= DMC: 3051
✖	= DMC: 3011
⊡	= DMC: 937
⊤	= DMC: 988

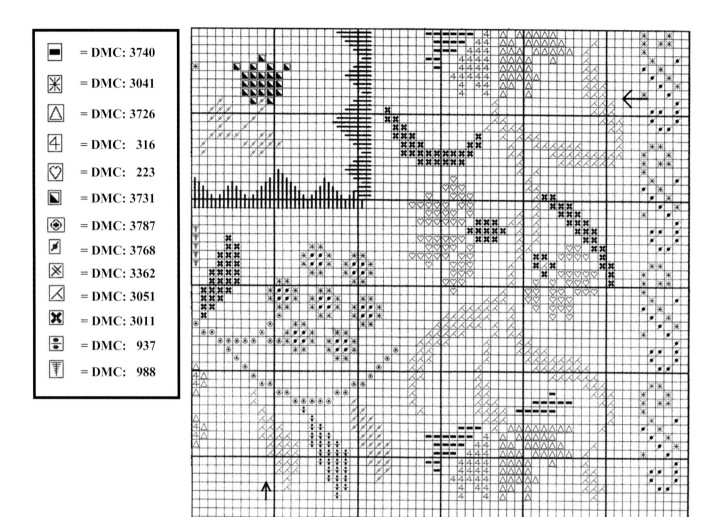

Chart Lower Right Hand Corner

<u>Each square on this chart represents two threads of fabric</u>

tpi = threads per inch

Refer to the frontispiece for additional detail

All cross stitch is worked using one thread of stranded cotton. For additional information on this refer to page 39.

The saw tooth satin stitch is worked using 1 thread of stranded cotton 3362 for linen with a thread count of 31 - 35tpi, 2 threads for 28 - 30tpi.

Large Floral Border Charts

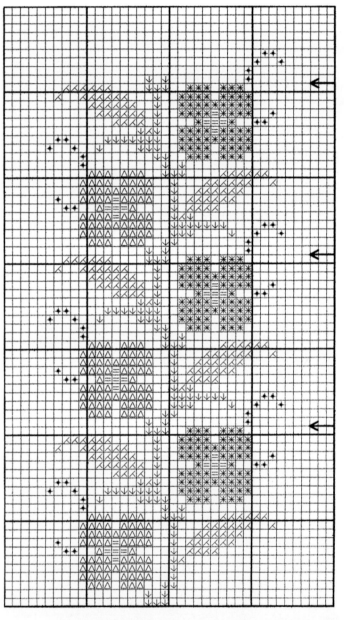

⌘	= DMC: 3041
△	= DMC: 3726
✚	= DMC: 832
⊟	= DMC: 3822
↓	= DMC: 3787
⧄	= DMC: 3051

Chart down left hand side of Sampler - Pansy border

Each square on this chart represents two threads of fabric

Arrows indicate pattern repeat

Refer to the frontispiece for additional detail

All cross stitch is worked using one thread of stranded cotton. For additional information on this refer to page 39.

▬	= DMC: 3740
△	= DMC: 3726
4	= DMC: 316
♡	= DMC: 223
◺	= DMC: 3051
✖	= DMC: 3011

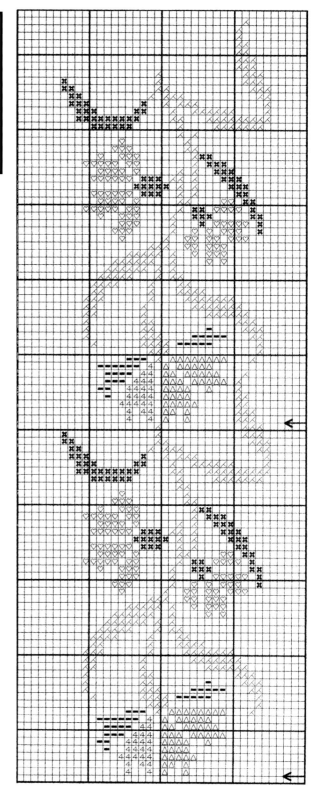

Chart down right hand side of Sampler – Carnation with long leaves

Each square on this chart represents two threads of fabric
Arrows indicate pattern repeat
Refer to the frontispiece for additional detail

All cross stitch is worked using one thread of stranded cotton. For additional information on this refer to page 39.

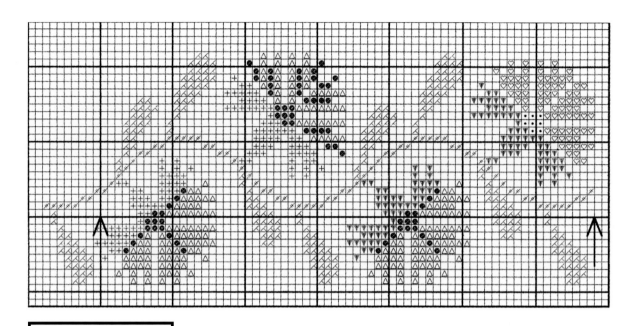

◆	= DMC: 3802
△	= DMC: 3726
♡	= DMC: 223
⊗	= DMC: 778
⊠	= DMC: 3362
◹	= DMC: 3051
⊤	= DMC: 988
⊞	= DMC: 471

Chart across the top of the Sampler - Carnation with short leaves

<u>Each square on this chart represents two threads of fabric</u>

Arrows indicate pattern repeat

Refer to the frontispiece for additional detail

All cross stitch is worked using one thread of stranded cotton. For additional information on this refer to page 39.

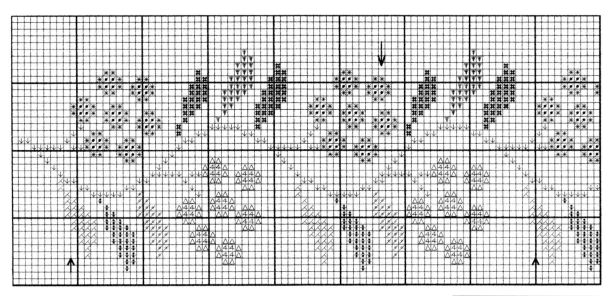

✳	= DMC: 3041
△	= DMC: 3726
4	= DMC: 316
↓	= DMC: 3787
⚡	= DMC: 3768
⊠	= DMC: 3362
◿	= DMC: 3051
⊠	= DMC: 3011
⊡	= DMC: 937
⊤	= DMC: 988

Chart across the base of the Sampler - Small Daisy border

<u>Each square on this chart represents two threads of fabric</u>
Arrows indicate pattern repeat
Refer to the frontispiece for additional detail

All cross stitch is worked using one thread of stranded cotton. For additional information on this refer to page 39.

To fit this pattern in I had to make a minor adjustment to the vine - the arrow at the top of the chart indicates this. You will note that the vine is worked with one stitch directly above the previous one - not diagonally above it.

Nine Inner Sections

Blocks 1 - 9

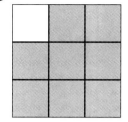

Block 1 - row of cherries across the top

Each square on this chart represents two threads of fabric

tpi = threads per inch

Refer to the colour photograph page 43 for additional detail

All cross stitch is worked using one thread of stranded cotton. For additional information on this refer to page 39.

The saw tooth satin stitch is worked using 1 thread of stranded cotton 3362 for linen with a thread count of 31 - 35tpi, 2 threads for linen 28 - 30tpi.

The satin stitch borders between the blocks are stitched using 1 thread of stranded cotton 3052 for linen with a thread count of 31- 35tpi, 2 threads for linen 28 - 30tpi.

Diamond area indicates overlap from previous section

Lower satin stitch pattern shown in full page 64.

▬	= DMC: 3740
✳	= DMC: 3041
●	= DMC: 3802
△	= DMC: 3726
4	= DMC: 316
♡	= DMC: 223
◣	= DMC: 3731
╱	= DMC: 778
✚	= DMC: 832
☰	= DMC: 3822
◇	= DMC: 924
◩	= DMC: 3768
✖	= DMC: 3011
↓	= DMC: 3787
⊠	= DMC: 3362
◹	= DMC: 3051
⊤	= DMC: 988

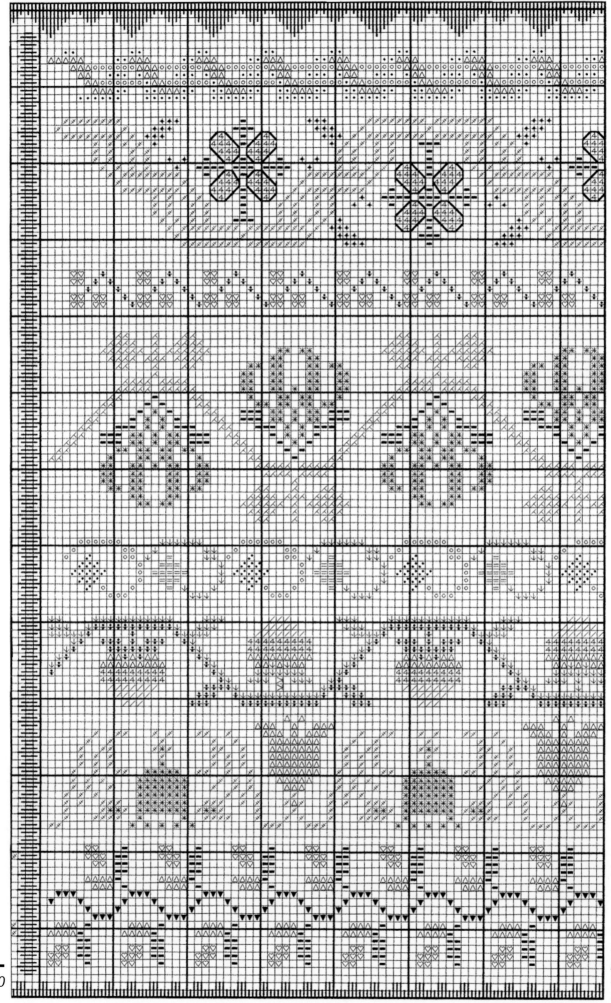

Lower satin stitch pattern shown in full page 64.

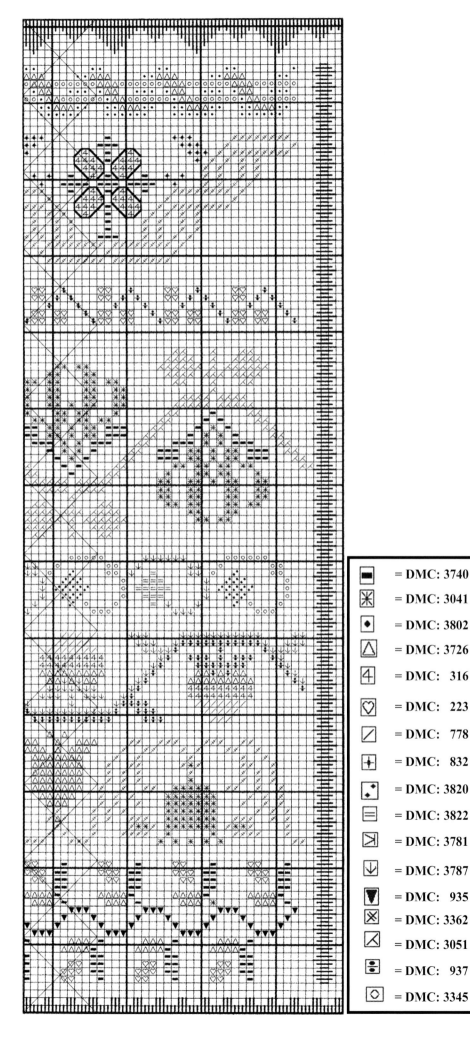

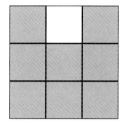

Block 2 - Pink and green winding ribbons across the top

<u>Each square on this chart represents two threads of fabric</u>
tpi = threads per inch

Refer to the colour photograph page 44 for additional detail

All cross stitch is worked using one thread of stranded cotton. For additional information on this refer to page 39.

The saw tooth satin stitch is worked using 1 thread of stranded cotton 3362 for linen with a thread count of 31 - 35tpi, 2 threads for linen 28 - 30tpi.

The satin stitch borders between the blocks are stitched using 1 thread of stranded cotton 3052 for linen with a thread count of 31- 35tpi, 2 threads for linen 28 - 30tpi.

Band 2 - Back stitch or Holbein stitch is worked around each of the petals of the flowers using one thread of 3768.

Diamond area indicates overlap from previous section

■	= DMC: 3740
✳	= DMC: 3041
●	= DMC: 3802
△	= DMC: 3726
4	= DMC: 316
♡	= DMC: 223
╱	= DMC: 778
+	= DMC: 832
∴	= DMC: 3820
=	= DMC: 3822
⊠	= DMC: 3781
↓	= DMC: 3787
▼	= DMC: 935
⊠	= DMC: 3362
╲	= DMC: 3051
⊡	= DMC: 937
◇	= DMC: 3345

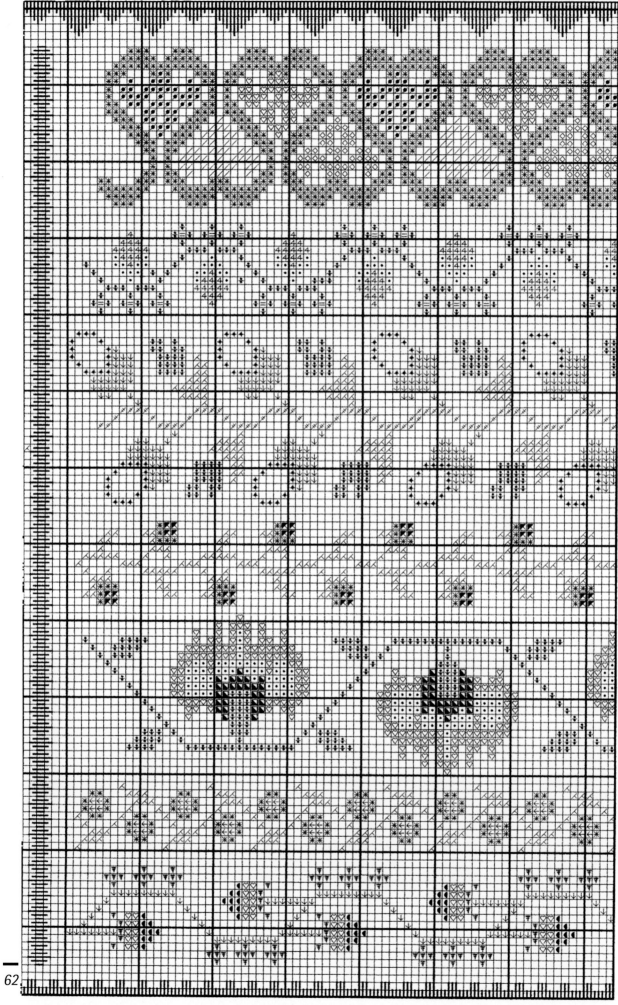

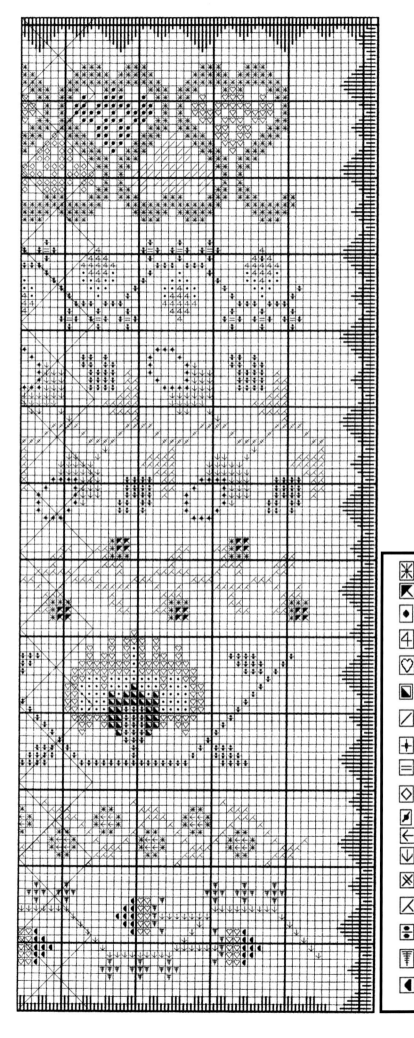

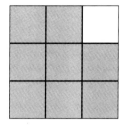

Block 3 Heart band across the top

<u>Each square on this chart represents two threads of fabric</u>
tpi = threads per inch

Refer to the colour photograph page 45 for additional detail

All cross stitch is worked using one thread of stranded cotton. For additional information on this refer to page 39.

The saw tooth satin stitch is worked using 1 thread of stranded cotton 3362 for linen with a thread count of 31 - 35tpi, 2 threads for linen 28 - 30tpi.

The satin stitch borders between the blocks are stitched using 1 thread of stranded cotton 3052 for linen with a thread count of 31- 35tpi, 2 threads for linen 28 - 30tpi.

Diamond area indicates overlap from previous section

Lower satin stitch pattern shown in full page 64.

✳	= DMC: 3041
◤	= DMC: 3042
●	= DMC: 3802
4	= DMC: 316
♡	= DMC: 223
◣	= DMC: 3731
/	= DMC: 778
+	= DMC: 832
=	= DMC: 3822
◇	= DMC: 924
◢	= DMC: 3768
←	= DMC: 926
↓	= DMC: 3787
⊠	= DMC: 3362
◹	= DMC: 3051
⦂	= DMC: 937
⊤	= DMC: 988
◖	= DMC: 3354

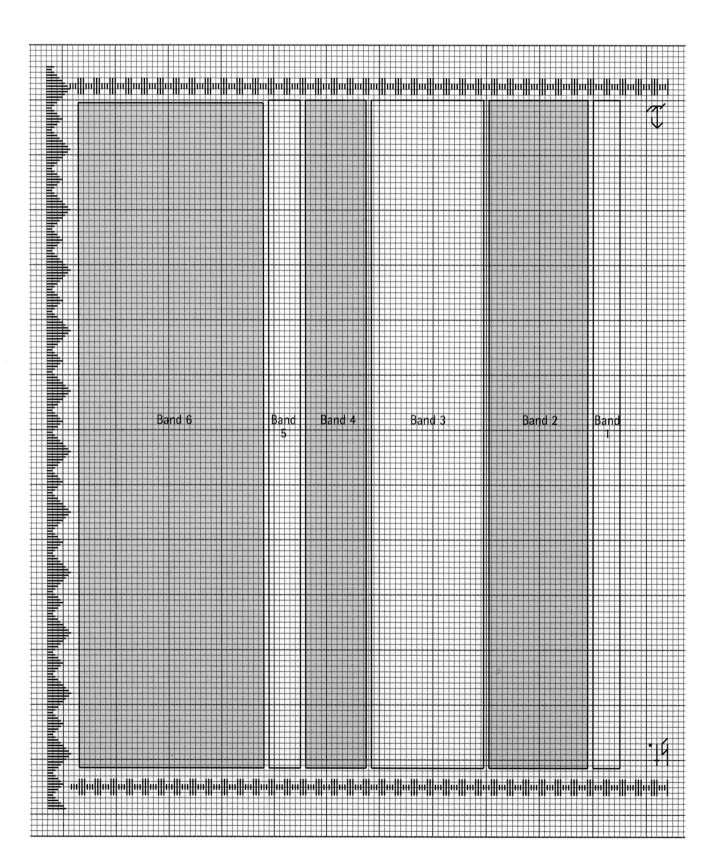

Block 4

To stitch Block 4 work from the centre towards the outside edge

tpi = threads per inch

Refer to the colour photograph page 46 for additional detail

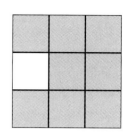

Alternative Sampler Verses

If you decide to choose different verses to the ones shown, work the lettering out on a piece of graph paper from the alphabets given on page 88. If the verses selected are longer than those shown you may need to drop one or two motifs. Always include your name and date on all your embroidery. More verses are given with Block 6.

If solid happiness we prize
Within our breast this jewel lies
And they are fools who roam.
The world has nothing to bestow;
From our own selves our joys must flow,
And that dear hut, our home.
  Nathaniel Cotton 1707-1788

No bird soars too high if he soars with his own wings.
  William Blake

All our talents increase in the using,
And every faculty, both good and bad,
Strengthens by exercise.
  Anne Bronte

Happiness is belonging not belongings.
  Unknown

Faith is to believe what we do not see,
And the reward of this faith is to see what we believe.
  St Augustine

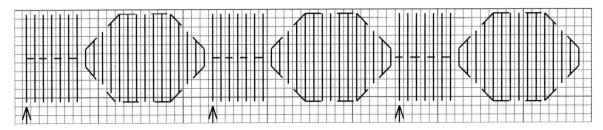

On this chart, <u>each line represents one thread</u>. tpi = threads per inch

Band 1

Arrows indicate pattern repeats.

The rounded shapes on this narrow satin stitch band are stitched using one thread of coton a broder 16 642 for linen with a thread count of 31 - 35tpi) (three threads of stranded cotton for linen 28 - 30tpi). They are then outlined in back stitch using one thread of 3052.

The connecting blocks are worked in satin stitch using two threads of 3052 for linen with a thread count of 31 - 35tpi (three threads for linen 28 - 30tpi). Note each stitch covers five threads - the dashed line at the centre of the blocks indicates the end of each stitch.

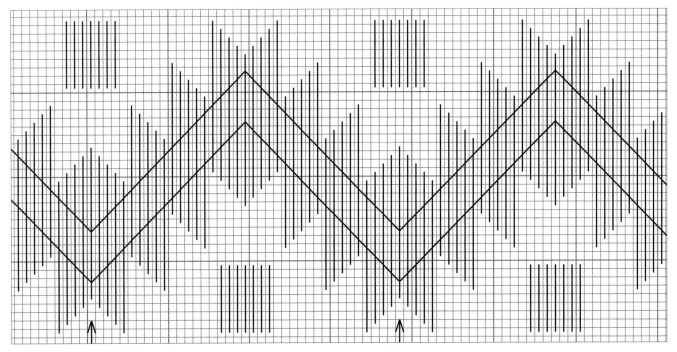

On this chart, <u>each line represents one thread</u>. tpi = threads per inch

Band 2

Arrows indicate pattern repeats.

This design is worked in two stages. Satin stitch the central zig zag line using one thread of coton a broder 16 642 for linen with a thread count of 31 - 35tpi, (three threads of stranded cotton for linen 28-30tpi). The diagonal lines running along each side of the central zig zag indicate the end point of each stitch - they are not stitched. The satin stitch triangles and blocks are worked using two threads of stranded cotton 3052 for linen with a thread count of 31 - 35tpi (three threads of stranded cotton for linen 28 - 30tpi).

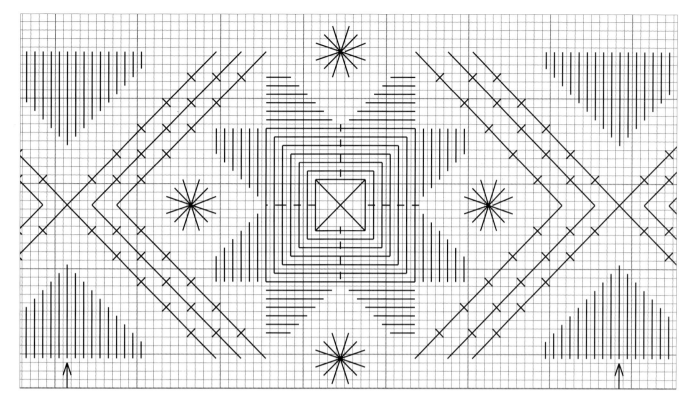

On this chart, <u>each line represents one thread</u>. tpi = threads per inch

Band 3

Arrows indicate pattern repeats.

This band is an interesting combination of ribbon stitch for texture, satin stitch for sheen and eyelets for contrast.

The ribbon stitch is worked using one thread of coton a broder 16 642 for all weights of linen and each stitch is worked up and over **three** threads. The short lines intersecting the diagonal lines indicate the end of each stitch.

The eyelets are worked on all weights of linen using one thread of stranded cotton 3052. Note these are circular eyelets, not one stitch is worked on the straight of the material. Remember to use a stiletto to create a perfect eyelet, see page 21.

All the satin stitch is worked using two threads of stranded cotton 3052 on linen with a thread count of 31 - 35tpi, (three threads of stranded cotton for linen 28 - 30tpi.). The dashed lines in the star indicates the end of each stitch. A simple eyelet is worked in the centre of each star using one thread of stranded 3052 for all linens.

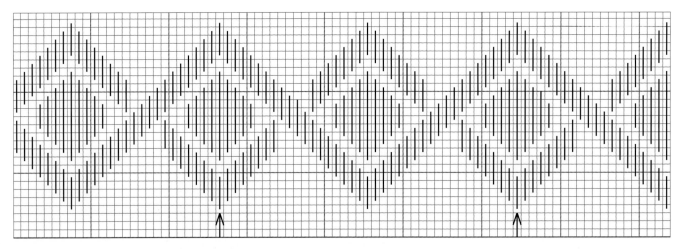

On this chart, <u>each line represents one thread</u>. tpi = threads per inch

Band 4

Arrows indicate pattern repeats.

All stitching is worked using two threads of stranded cotton 3052 for linen with a thread count of 31 -
35tpi, (three threads of stranded cotton for linen 28- 30 tpi). Work the unbroken line of satin stitch first.

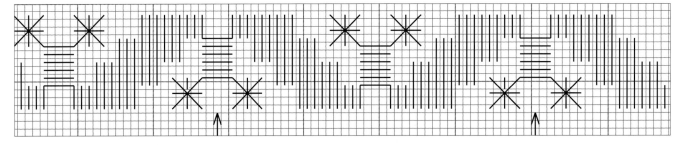

On this chart, <u>each line represents one thread</u>. tpi = threads per inch

Band 5

Arrows indicate pattern repeats.

This narrow band combines satin stitch and square eyelets. The satin stitch is worked first using one thread
of coton a broder 16 642 for linen with a thread count of 31 - 35tpi and three threads of stranded cotton
for linen with a thread count of 28 - 30tpi. Use the same thread to work the square eyelets.

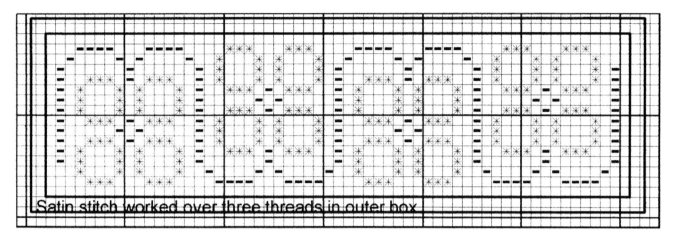

Satin stitch worked over three threads in outer box

━ = Needleweaving

✳ = Ghost Stitch

Band 6

There are two designs given for this area - a panel of filet embroidery or satin stitch designs. Choose whichever panel you prefer, both will look most attractive on your completed sampler.

The Filet Panel

On this chart <u>each square and each line represent two threads.</u>

(Each line equals two threads whipped together and each gap equals two threads removed.)

Filet embroidery was extremely popular in the sixteenth and seventeenth centuries when only the nobility were allowed to wear lace. Filet embroidery enabled others to create the 'look' of lace. Delicate and attractive, this technique is a satisfying and enjoyable technique to master. If you have not previously stitched this technique refer to page 27 for detailed instructions on working the design given here. Read through all the instructions before you begin to stitch and remember to use an embroidery hoop at all times.

The satin stitch outlining the entire design area is worked using coton a broder 16 medium mole 642 and is worked over **three** threads. It is centred in the area available and the outer edge is stitched two threads from the top of the satin stitch saw tooth design.

The whipping is worked using one thread of stranded cotton 642. The needle weaving is worked using one thread of coton a broder 16 642 and the ghost stitch is worked using one thread of coton a broder 25 642 for all linens

The design is 59 gaps wide and 16 gaps high.
Alternatively this panel may be replaced with the satin stitch designs given on pags 70-71.

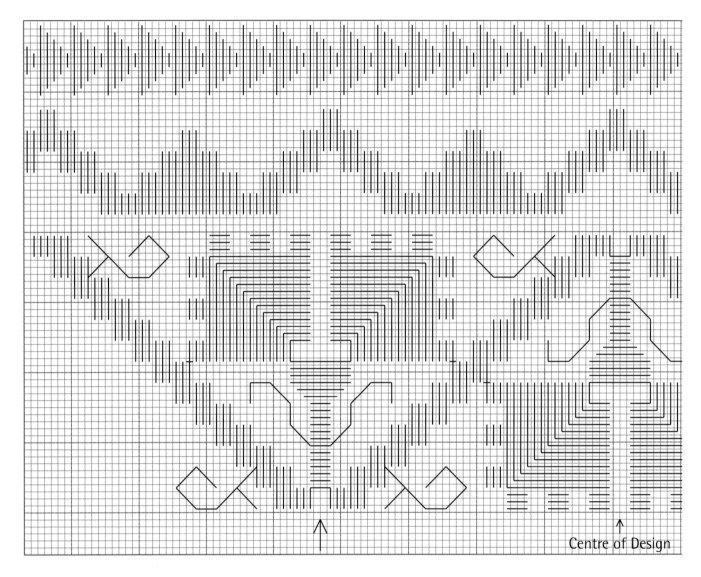

Centre of Design

On this chart, <u>each line represents one thread</u>. tpi = threads per inch
Alternative Band 6 is made up of Bands 6, 7 & 8
Band 8 *Arrows indicate pattern repeats - the centre of the design is also indicated.*
There are three bands to be used in this area, bands 6, 7 and 8. The stylized carnation design (band 8) is
centred and for this reason it is best if you stitch this design first. It is stitched two threads from the top
of the satin stitch saw tooth design, start at the centre and work out to each edge. The main zig zag
running through the design and the flower stem are stitched using coton a broder 16 642 for linen with a
thread count of 31 - 35 tpi (three threads of stranded cotton for linen 28 - 30tpi). The flower head is
worked using two threads of stranded cotton 3052 for linen with a thread count of 31 - 35 tpi (three
threads of stranded cotton for linen 28 - 30tpi) as is the back stitch.

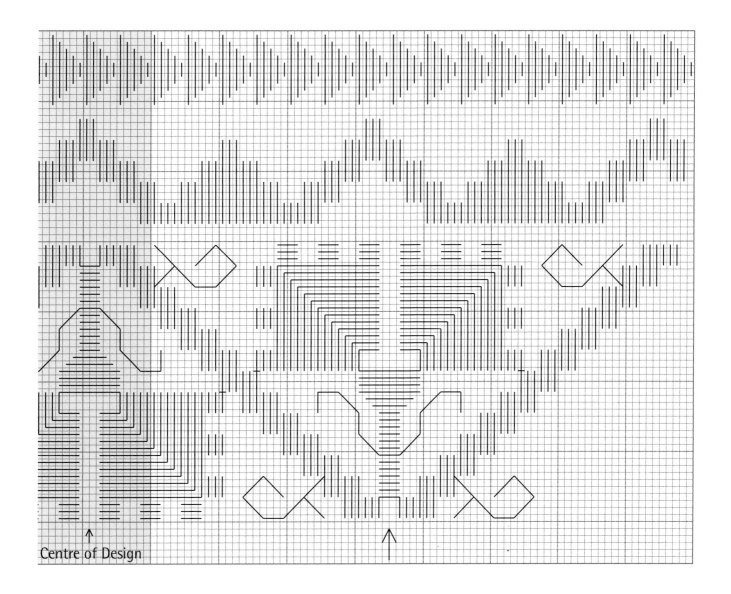

Centre of Design

Band 7 Block and Zig Zag Centre this design above band 8 - refer to the chart for the starting position. It is stitch using coton a broder 16 642 for linen with a thread count of 31 - 35tpi (three threads of stranded cotton for linen 28 - 30tpi) throughout.

Band 6 is worked with triangles of 642 alternating with triangles of 3052. Start this design in the centre also. For the first triangle use coton a broder 16 642 for linen with a thread count of 31 - 35tpi (three threads of stranded cotton for 28 - 30tpi) and for the second triangle use two threads of stranded cotton 3052 for linen with a thread count of 31 - 35tpi (three threads of stranded cotton for linen 28 - 30tpi)

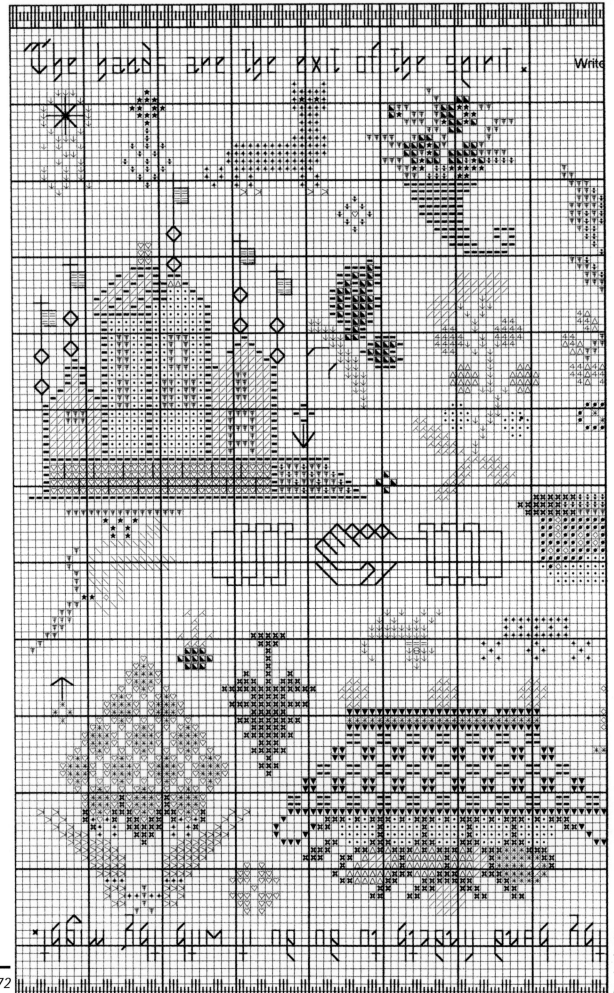

The hands are the exit of the spirit.

Lower satin stitch pattern shown in full page 64

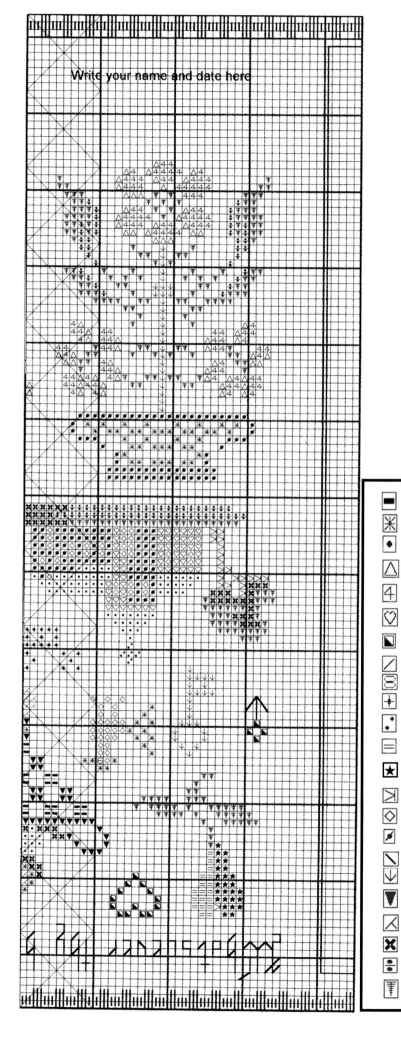

Write your name and date here

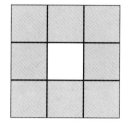

Block 5 Centre

<u>Each square on this chart represents two threads of fabric</u> tpi = threads per inch

Refer to the colour photograph page 46 for additional detail

All cross stitch is worked using one thread of stranded cotton. For additional information on this refer to page 39.

The spokes of the spinning wheel are straight stitches worked using one thread of 3787.

The flagpoles and outlines round the flags on the large house are worked using one thread of 677. Back or Holbein stitch is worked in the lower area of the house to create the illusion of bricks, it is stitched using one thread of 3740.

The stems of all the small flowers worked in this area are stitched using one thread of 937
The clasped hands are worked in back or Holbein stitch using one thread of 3362.

Diamond area indicates overlap from previous section

■	= DMC: 3740
✳	= DMC: 3041
●	= DMC: 3802
△	= DMC: 3726
4	= DMC: 316
♡	= DMC: 223
◣	= DMC: 3731
╱	= DMC: 778
⊗	= DMC: 928
✚	= DMC: 832
⬩	= DMC: 3820
=	= DMC: 3822
★	= DMC: 677
⊳	= DMC: 3781
◇	= DMC: 924
⬚	= DMC: 3768
╲	= DMC: 517
↓	= DMC: 3787
▼	= DMC: 935
⟋	= DMC: 3051
✖	= DMC: 3011
⊟	= DMC: 937
⊤	= DMC: 988

73

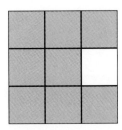

Block 6
To stitch Block 4 work from the
centre towards the outside edge
tpi = threads per inch

*Refer to the colour photograph
page 47 for additional detail*

Alternative Sampler Verses

*The greater part
Our happiness or misery
Depends on our dispositions
And not on our circumstances*
    Martha Washington

They are able because they think they are able.
    Vergil Aeneid

*In matters of style, swim with the current;
in matters of principle, stand like a rock.*
    Thomas Jefferson

There is nothing either good or bad, but thinking makes it so.
    William Shakespeare

Great works are performed not by strength but by perseverance.
    Samuel Johnson

In youth we learn; in age we understand
    Marie Ebner-Eschenbach

The future belongs to those who believe in the beauty of their dreams
    Eleanor Roosevelt.

Chance favours the prepared mind.
    Louis Pasteur

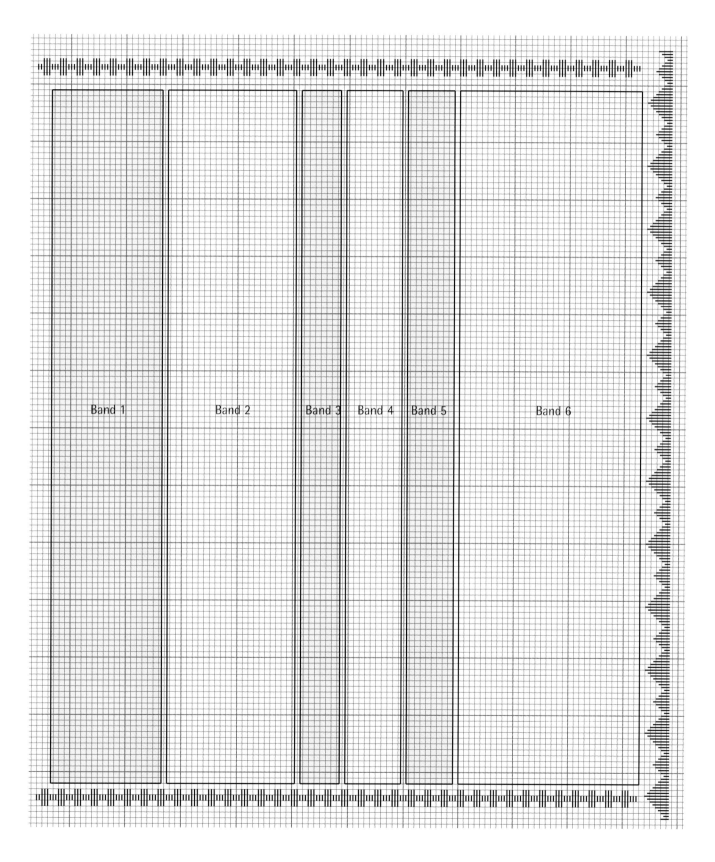

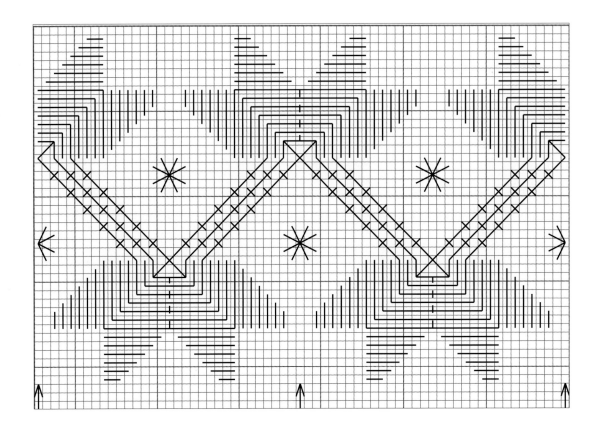

On this chart, <u>each line represents one thread</u>. tpi = threads per inch

Band 1

Arrows indicate pattern repeats.

Ribbon stitch and satin stitch are combined in this design in subtle shades of green and taupe. The ribbon stitch is worked using one thread of coton a broder 25 642 for linen with a thread count of 31 - 35tpi (three threads of stranded cotton for linen 28 - 30tpi). Each stitch is worked up and over two threads. The short lines intersecting the diagonal lines indicate the end of each stitch.

The satin stitch stars are worked using two threads of stranded cotton 3052 for linen with a thread count of 31 - 35 tpi (three threads of stranded cotton for linen 28 - 30tpi). The dashed lines in the stars indicate the end of each stitch. A circular eyelet is worked between the stars using one thread of stranded 3052 on all linens, don't forget to use the stiletto for a perfect circular eyelet every time!

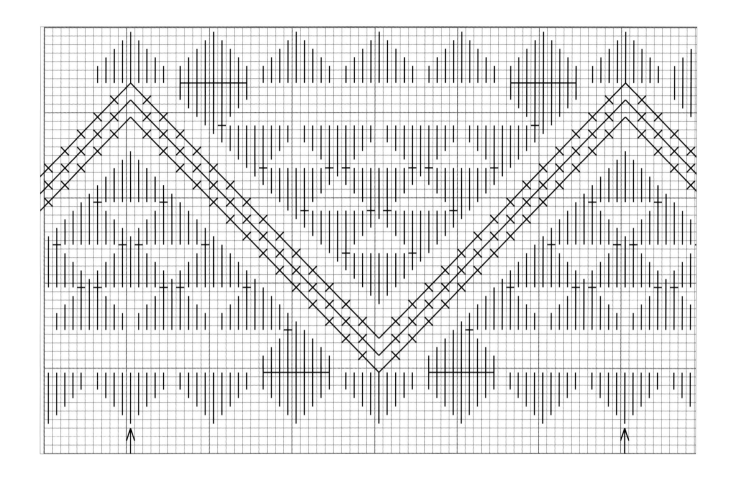

On this chart, <u>each line represents one thread</u>. tpi = threads per inch

Band 2

Arrows indicate pattern repeats.

This design is worked in two stages. Work the ribbon stitch running through the design first, using one thread of coton a broder 16 642 for all weights of linen and working each stitch over two threads. The short lines intersecting the diagonal lines indicate the end of each stitch. The satin stitch triangles are worked using two threads of stranded cotton 3052 for linen with a thread count of 31 - 35tpi (three threads of stranded cotton for linen 28 - 30tpi). The horizontal lines crossing the vertical lines indicate the end of each stitch.

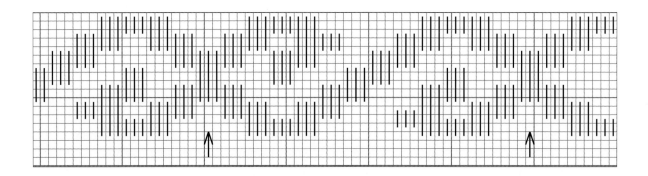

On this chart, <u>each line represents one thread</u>. tpi = threads per inch

Band 3

Arrows indicate pattern repeats.

This is an attractive small repeating pattern. It is worked in satin stitch using two threads of stranded cotton 3052 for linen with a thread count of 31 - 35tpi and three threads of stranded cotton for linen with a thread count of 28 - 30tpi.

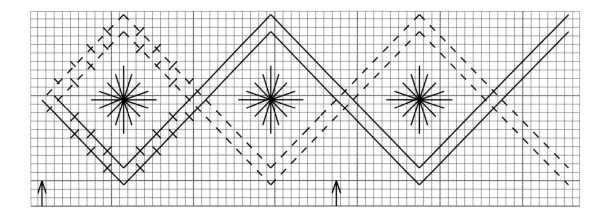

On this chart, <u>each line represents one thread</u>. tpi = threads per inch

Band 4

Arrows indicate pattern repeats.

This is a combination of ribbon stitch and eyelets. The ribbon stitch is worked in two journeys and is only two stitches wide. Complete the ribbon stitch along the dashed line first. It is worked throughout in coton a broder 25 642 for linen with a thread count of 31 - 35tpi but using coton a broder 16 for linen with a thread count of 28 - 30tpi. The short lines intersecting the diagonal lines in the first diamond indicate the end of each stitch.

The eyelets are worked on all linens using one thread of stranded cotton 3052.

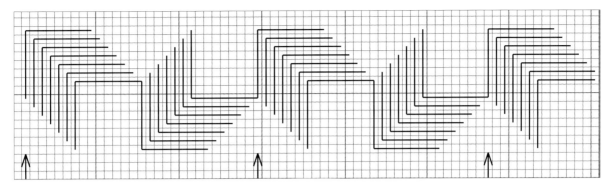

Band 5 On this chart, <u>each line represents one thread</u>. tpi = threads per inch
Arrows indicate pattern repeats.
This is a very simple but very effective design. Stitch using one thread of coton a broder 16 642 for linen with a thread count of 31 - 35tpi but use three threads of stranded cotton for linen with 28 - 30tpi.

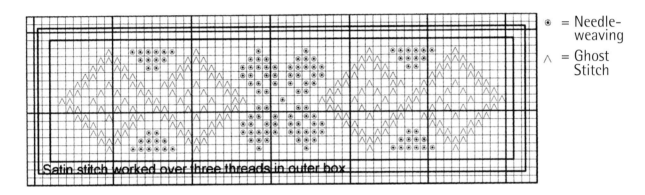

⊛ = Needle-
weaving

∧ = Ghost
Stitch

Band 6
There are two designs given for this area - a panel of filet embroidery or satin stitch designs. Choose whichever panel you prefer, both will look most attractive on your completed sampler.

The Filet Panel
On this chart <u>each square and each line represent two threads.</u>
(Each line equals two threads whipped together and each gap equals two threads removed.)
Filet embroidery was extremely popular in the sixteenth and seventeenth centuries when only the nobility were allowed to wear lace. Filet embroidery enabled others to create the 'look' of lace. Delicate and attractive, this technique is a satisfying and enjoyable technique to master. If you have not previously stitched this technique refer to page 27 for detailed instructions on working the design given here. Read through all the instructions before you begin to stitch and remember to use an embroidery hoop at all times.

The design is 59 gaps wide and 15 gaps high. The satin stitch outlining the entire design area is worked using coton a broder 16 medium mole 642 and is worked over **three** threads. It is centred in the area available and the outer edge is stitched two threads from the top of the satin stitch saw tooth design.

The whipping is worked using one thread of stranded cotton 642. The needle weaving is worked using one thread of coton a broder 16 642 and the ghost stitch is worked using one thread of coton a broder 25 642. *Alternatively this panel may be replaced with the satin stitch designs given on pages 80-81.*

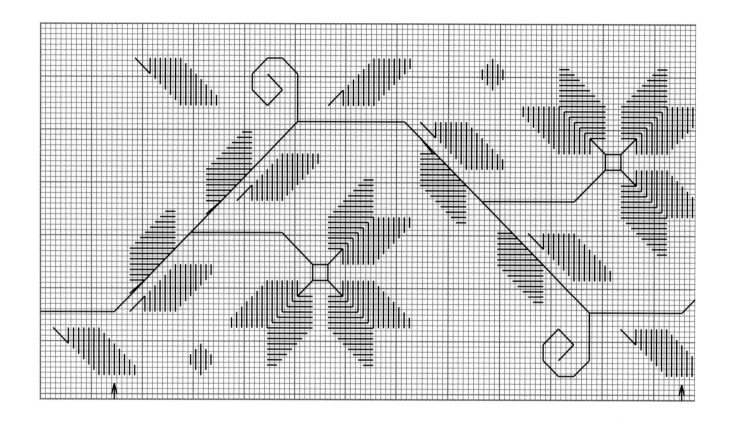

On this chart, <u>each line represents one thread</u>. tpi = threads per inch

Alternative Band 6

Arrows indicate pattern repeats.

It is stitched two threads above the top of the satin stitch saw tooth design. Start this design at the left hand side of the area working from the chart.

The vine and stalks are worked in Holbein stitch using coton a broder 16 642 on all linens. Leaves and all satin stitched areas are worked using two threads of stranded cotton 3052 for linen with 31 - 35tpi and three threads of stranded cotton for linen with a thread count of 28 - 30tpi.

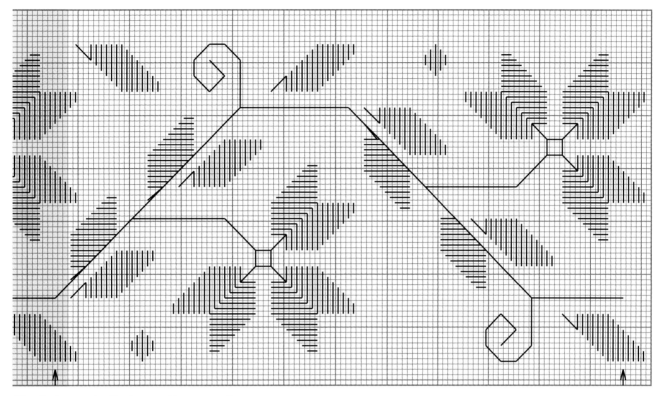

Shaded area indicates pattern overlap.

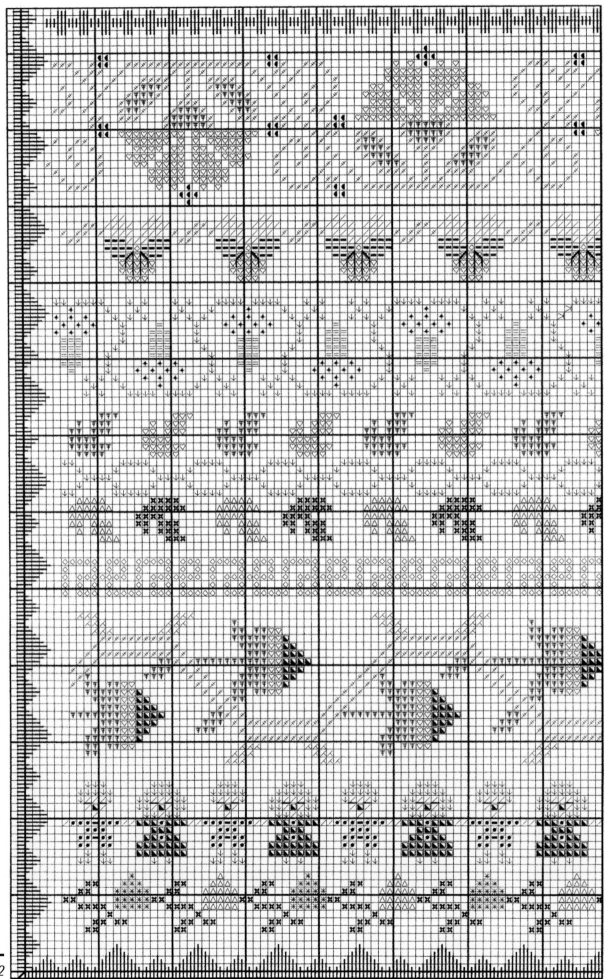

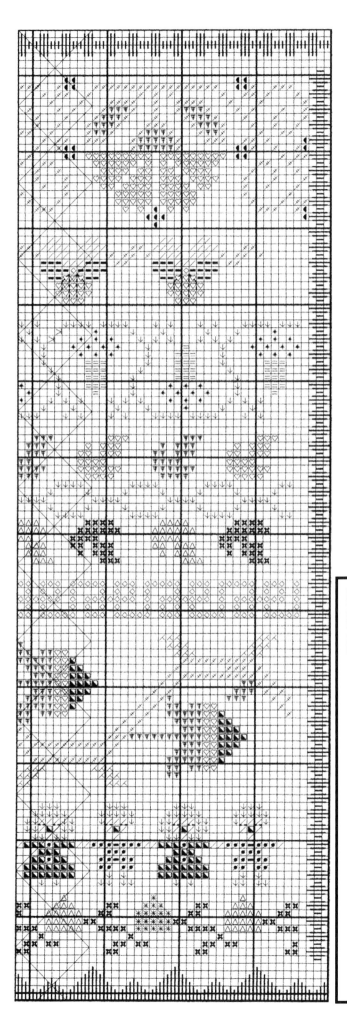

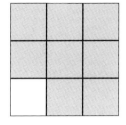

Block 7 Three large pink carnations across the top

<u>Each square on this chart represents two threads of fabric</u>

Refer to the colour photograph page 48 for additional detail

All cross stitch is worked using one thread of stranded cotton. For additional information on this refer to page 39.

The saw tooth satin stitch is worked using 1 thread of stranded cotton 3362 for linen with a thread count of 31 - 35tpi, 2 threads for linen 28 - 30tpi.

The satin stitch borders between the blocks are stitched using 1 thread of stranded cotton 3052 for linen with a thread count of 31- 35tpi, 2 threads for linen 28 - 30tpi.

Diamond area indicates overlap from previous section

■	= DMC: 3740
✳	= DMC: 3041
△	= DMC: 3726
♡	= DMC: 223
◣	= DMC: 3731
╱	= DMC: 778
✚	= DMC: 832
═	= DMC: 3822
▷	= DMC: 3781
◇	= DMC: 924
◪	= DMC: 3768
←	= DMC: 926
↓	= DMC: 3787
☒	= DMC: 3362
◺	= DMC: 3051
✖	= DMC: 3011
☗	= DMC: 988
◀	= DMC: 3354

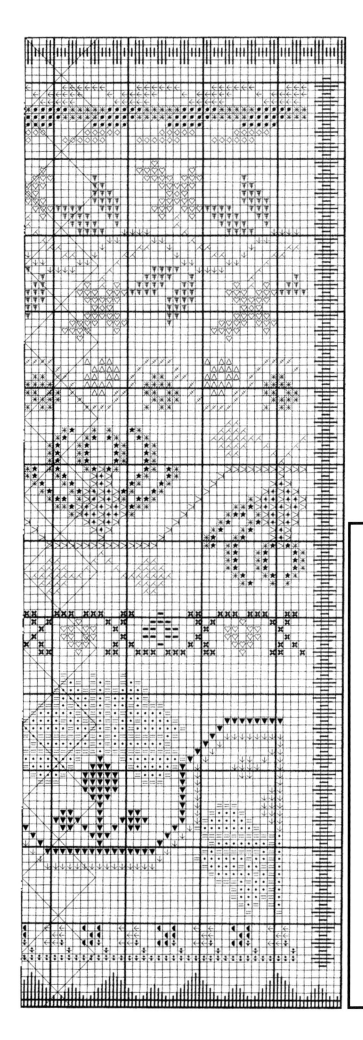

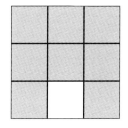

Block 8 Shades of blue twisting ribbons

<u>Each square on this chart represents two threads of fabric</u>

Refer to the colour photograph page 49 for additional detail

All cross stitch is worked using one thread of stranded cotton. For additional information on this refer to page 39.

The saw tooth satin stitch is worked using 1 thread of stranded cotton 3362 for linen with a thread count of 31 - 35tpi, 2 threads for linen 28 - 30tpi.

The satin stitch borders between the blocks are stitched using 1 thread of stranded cotton 3052 for linen with a thread count of 31- 35tpi, 2 threads for linen 28 - 30tpi.

Diamond area indicates overlap from previous section

■	= DMC: 3740
✳	= DMC: 3041
◆	= DMC: 3802
△	= DMC: 3726
♡	= DMC: 223
✛	= DMC: 832
⊟	= DMC: 3822
★	= DMC: 677
↗	= DMC: 3781
◇	= DMC: 924
⬚	= DMC: 3768
←	= DMC: 926
↓	= DMC: 3787
▼	= DMC: 935
⊠	= DMC: 3362
◩	= DMC: 3051
✖	= DMC: 3011
⊡	= DMC: 937
⊤	= DMC: 988
◀	= DMC: 3354

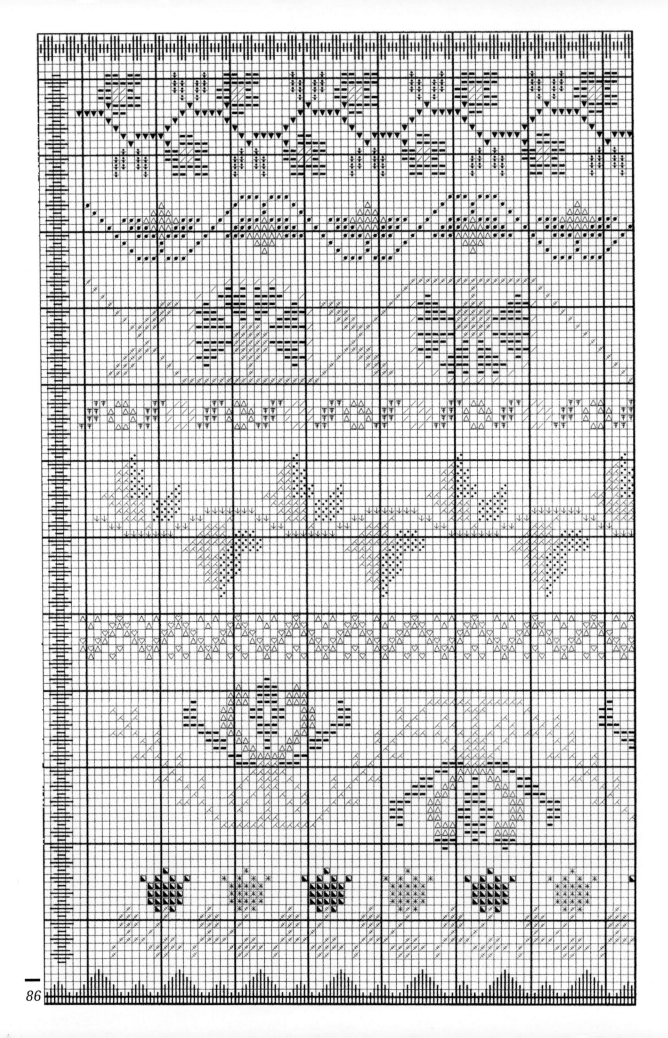

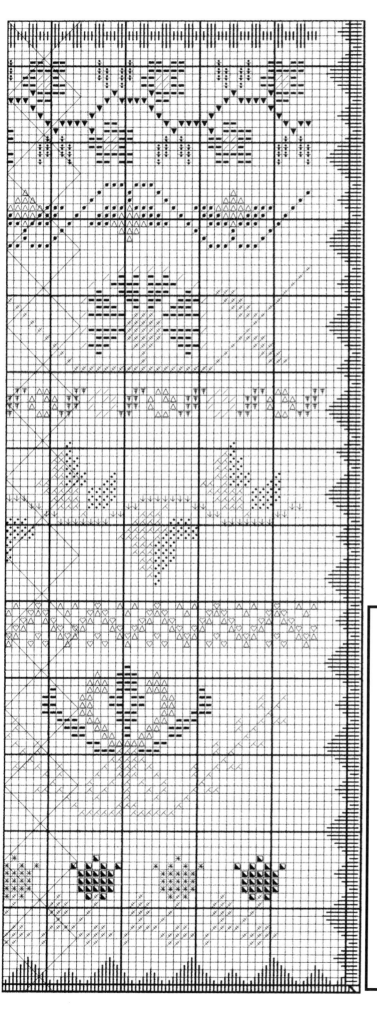

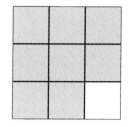

Block 9 Blue mauve small flowers across the top

<u>Each square on this chart represents two threads of fabric</u>

Refer to the colour photograph page 50 for additional detail

All cross stitch is worked using one thread of stranded cotton. For additional information on this refer to page 39.

The saw tooth satin stitch is worked using 1 thread of stranded cotton 3362 for linen with a thread count of 31 - 35tpi, 2 threads for linen 28 - 30tpi.

The satin stitch borders between the blocks are stitched using 1 thread of stranded cotton 3052 for linen with a thread count of 31- 35tpi, 2 threads for linen 28 - 30tpi.

Diamond area indicates overlap from previous section

▬	= DMC: 3740
✳	= DMC: 3041
△	= DMC: 3726
♡	= DMC: 223
◣	= DMC: 3731
⁄	= DMC: 778
⬧	= DMC: 3820
⬜	= DMC: 3768
↓	= DMC: 3787
▼	= DMC: 935
⨯	= DMC: 3362
⟋	= DMC: 3051
▣	= DMC: 937
▼	= DMC: 988

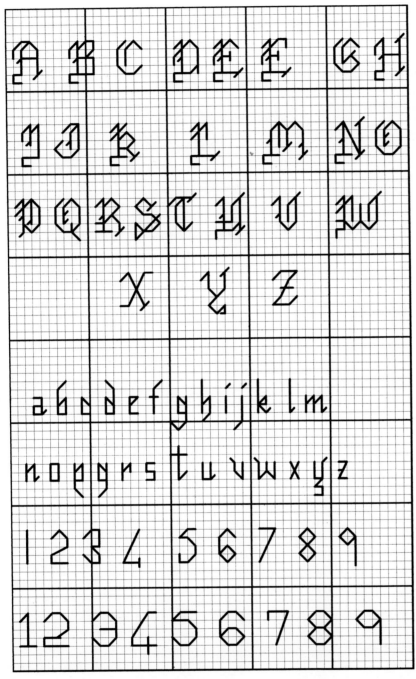

Alphabet & Numerals

<u>Each square on this chart represents two threads of fabric</u>

This is worked in Holbein or back stitch and is stitched using one thread of stranded cotton in the colour of your choice.